SURREY WATERWAYS

P.A.L. VINE

1987

Design – Deborah Goodridge

First published November 1987

ISBN 0 906520 517

Published by Middleton Press
Easebourne Lane
Midhurst, West Sussex
GU29 9AZ
☎ 073 081 3169

Printed & bound by Biddles Ltd,
Guildford and Kings Lynn

CONTENTS

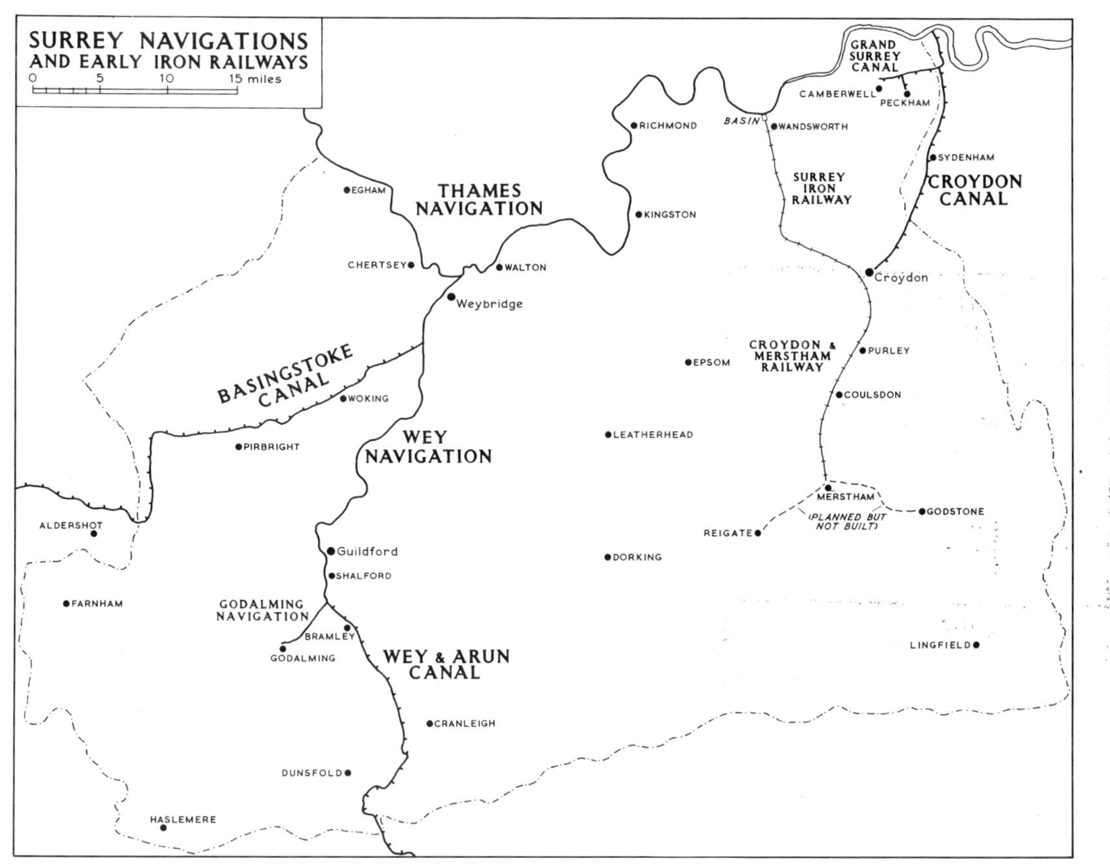

ACKNOWLEDGEMENTS

I am very grateful indeed to those who have kindly assisted me or have lent me photographs, and in particular to Miss Kay Bowen, Bromley Local History Library, Michael Cardew, Croydon Local History Library, The Daily Telegraph, Bob Dawes, Clive Durley, Dendy Easton, Gerald Griffith, Guildford Muniment Room, Guildford Museum, Guildhall Library, Charles Hadfield, Miss Diana Hanks, Dieter Jebens, Mrs. Sonia Jebens, J. Jennings, Mrs. Avril Lansdell (curator of the Weybridge Museum), Hugh McKnight, Vic Mitchell, Montagu Motor Museum, Museum of London, David Robinson, Ronald Russell, Dr. Roger Sellman, Aubrey Slaughter, the late W.H. Smart, Southwark Local Studies Library, the late Harry W. Stevens, The Surrey Advertiser, The Surrey & Hampshire Canal Society, Surrey Record Office, Kingston upon Thames, W.J. Thomson, Miss Edwina Vine, R.A. Williams, John Wood (Hon. Secretary of the Wey & Arun Canal Trust), Dr. F.W. Wright, Young & Co's Brewery, Wandsworth.

HISTORICAL BACKGROUND

For centuries the River Thames and the Port of London formed the vital artery of Britain's commerce. The Thames was never made navigable for it had always been so although above its tidal reaches boats were much impeded by fish dams and mill weirs into which were incorporated flash locks. Not until 1635 was the river considered navigable for barges as far as Oxford.

Although the Thames forms the northern boundary of Surrey, this book concentrates on the county's waterways which were made navigable. Its rivers are all tributaries of the Thames but only the Wey was in fact artificially improved. In spite of many proposals for new waterways during the canal era, only four were in fact built. The Basingstoke Canal of whose course little more than one third is in Surrey but in which county lie 28 of the waterway's 29 locks. The Grand Surrey Canal which was planned to reach Mitcham from Rotherhithe but which in fact only went as far as Camberwell. The Croydon Canal which was built from the Grand Surrey Canal to Forest Hill, Selhurst and Croydon and which was in competition with the Surrey Iron Railway for some twenty-five years. Lastly in point of time came the Wey & Arun Junction Canal, alias the Surrey and Sussex Canal, which ran nine miles to the south of Shalford before crossing into Sussex en route for the Arun valley and the English Channel.

Several important Surrey rivers were never made navigable although various proposals were put forward. The River Mole (30 miles long) was one of the earliest to be considered and in 1664 an Act was granted to build a waterway from Reigate to the Thames. In 1810 Richard Pottinger also proposed a navigation from Holmwood to Thames Ditton with cuttings to Stoke d'Abernon, Cobham and Esher. In the 1780's a canal 18 feet wide and 5 feet deep to take 30 ton barges was projected from Ewell to Kingston with wharves by the corn and gunpowder mills on the Hogsmill river. The estimated cost was £5708 but the idea was dropped. The many water-mills (in 1850 there were 14) on the fast flowing eleven mile long river Wandle precluded serious attempts to make it navigable. However James Easton produced a scheme for a canal from Wandsworth to Nine Elms in 1828 and plans

SUMMARY OF FACTS

Waterway	Terminal Points	Distance (miles)	No. Locks	Year Opened	To
Basingstoke Canal	Woodham-Basingstoke	$37\frac{1}{2}$	29	1791	Woking
				1792	Pyrford
				1793	Odiham
				1794	Basingstoke
Croydon Canal	New Cross-Croydon	$9\frac{1}{4}$	28	1809	Croydon
Godalming Navigation	Guildford-Godalming	$4\frac{1}{2}$	4	1763	Godalming
Grand Surrey Canal	Rotherhithe Camberwell	$3\frac{1}{8}$	2	1807	Grand Surrey Basin
				1810	Camberwell
	Peckham branch	$\frac{5}{8}$	none	1826	Peckham
Wandsworth Canal	Wandsworth Creek Ram Field	$\frac{3}{8}$	1	1802	Ram Field
Wey & Arun Junction Canal	Shalford Newbridge	$18\frac{1}{2}$	23	1815	Bramley
				1816	Newbridge
Wey Navigation	Weybridge Guildford	$15\frac{1}{4}$	12	1653	Guildford

were deposited in 1865 for a $2\frac{1}{2}$ mile canal with 2 locks parallel to the river from the Wandsworth Canal (built by the Surrey Iron Railway) to Plough Lane, Wimbledon.

Besides the Grand Imperial Ship Canal projected from London to Portsmouth in 1824, various canals were planned between the Thames and the English Channel which are described in London's Lost Route to the Sea (David & Charles 4th Edition 1986). Just as the Surrey Iron Railway was the world's first public railway, so the Croydon Canal was the first waterway to be taken over by a railway when it was closed in 1836.

The Wey Navigation, whose commercial utility lasted over a period of three hundrd years, was the most profitable of the Surrey waterways and played an important role in the development of trade to Guildford and Godalming. Its busiest period was in the 1830's when an average annual tonnage of 68,000 was carried compared with 25,000 on the Basingstoke Canal and 18,000 on the Wey & Arun Junction Canal. A century later between 1930 and 1936, 51,000 tons was still being carried annually. Railway competition caused the Wey & Arun to close in 1871 but the Basingstoke remained in commercial use until 1949, the Godalming Navigation until 1950 and the Wey Navigation until July 1969. The Wandsworth Canal ceased to be used about 1920 and the Grand Surrey Canal was closed with the abandonment of the Surrey Docks in 1971.

What is There to See Today?

The bed of the Croydon canal was utilized by the London & Croydon Railway Line opened in 1839. The odd relics which have survived are mentioned in the text. Although the Grand Surrey Canal was only closed in 1971, recent redevelopment has left equally few points of interest. However there are two interesting 19th century iron bridges and a milestone preserved on the Peckham branch. Much of the Basingstoke Canal has now been restored to how it appeared in the eighteenth century; particularly interesting is the Frimley flight of 14 locks, Deepcut and Frimley Aqueduct beneath which the trains from Waterloo to Basingstoke rush. Only the few miles beyond Greywell Tunnel remain difficult of access and a challenge to the countryside explorer seeking traces of the former channel, last used eighty years ago. The Surrey portion of the Wey & Arun Canal is less easy to trace as much of the canal bed between Shalford and Bramley has been filled in; however between Wonersh and the county boundary some sylvan reaches remain undisturbed both from the obliteration of new development and the new look of reclamation. The Wey Navigation, now owned by the National Trust, remains open for pleasure craft from Weybridge to Godalming. The best way to view this historic waterway is by boat and there are establishments at Farncombe, Guildford and further downstream offering a wide choice of boats for hire.

Year Commercial Traffic Ceased	To	Whether Navigable in 1987
1901	Basingstoke	Partially.
1919	Odiham	Anticipated
1920	Aldershot	reopening to
1949	Woking	Greywell in 1989
1836	Croydon	No
1925	Godalming	Yes
1950	Shalford.	
1971	Surrey Docks	No
1945	Camberwell	
1945	Peckham	
c1920	Ram Field	No
1871	Newbridge	No. Short
1872	Bramley	stretches for canoes only.
1958	Guildford	Yes
1969	Weybridge	

GRAND IMPERIAL SHIP CANAL PROJECT

This grandiose scheme to build a ship canal from London to Portsmouth in the eighteen twenties would have changed the face of Surrey had it come to pass. Planned to allow the largest ships of the line to sail from the Thames at Rotherhithe to the English Channel using ten locks each 300 feet long and 64 feet wide, it would have also entailed cuttings varying from 50 to 250 feet deep. Various routes were considered. The shortest (78 miles) proposed by Nicholas Cundy was considered too difficult; James Elmes' line (100 miles) via Croydon, far from easy due to the amount of excavation; and the longest (160 miles) via the river Medway, impracticable; John Rennie favoured a 86 mile line via Chessington and Guildford but estimated that the cost would be £6½ million. Although a bill was presented to the House of Commons in 1828, the Government were unwilling to support it on the grounds that it was not financially viable and the project died.

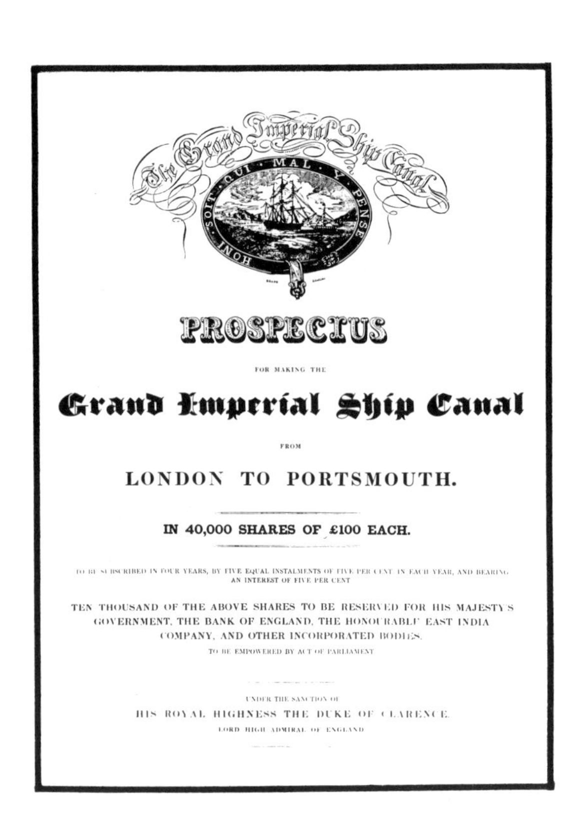
The Grand Imperial Ship Canal

HONI SOIT QUI MAL Y PENSE

PROSPECTUS

FOR MAKING THE

Grand Imperial Ship Canal

FROM

LONDON TO PORTSMOUTH.

IN 40,000 SHARES OF £100 EACH.

TO BE SUBSCRIBED IN FOUR YEARS, BY FIVE EQUAL INSTALMENTS OF FIVE PER CENT IN EACH YEAR, AND BEARING AN INTEREST OF FIVE PER CENT

TEN THOUSAND OF THE ABOVE SHARES TO BE RESERVED FOR HIS MAJESTY'S GOVERNMENT, THE BANK OF ENGLAND, THE HONOURABLE EAST INDIA COMPANY, AND OTHER INCORPORATED BODIES.

TO BE EMPOWERED BY ACT OF PARLIAMENT

UNDER THE SANCTION OF

HIS ROYAL HIGHNESS THE DUKE OF CLARENCE.

LORD HIGH ADMIRAL OF ENGLAND

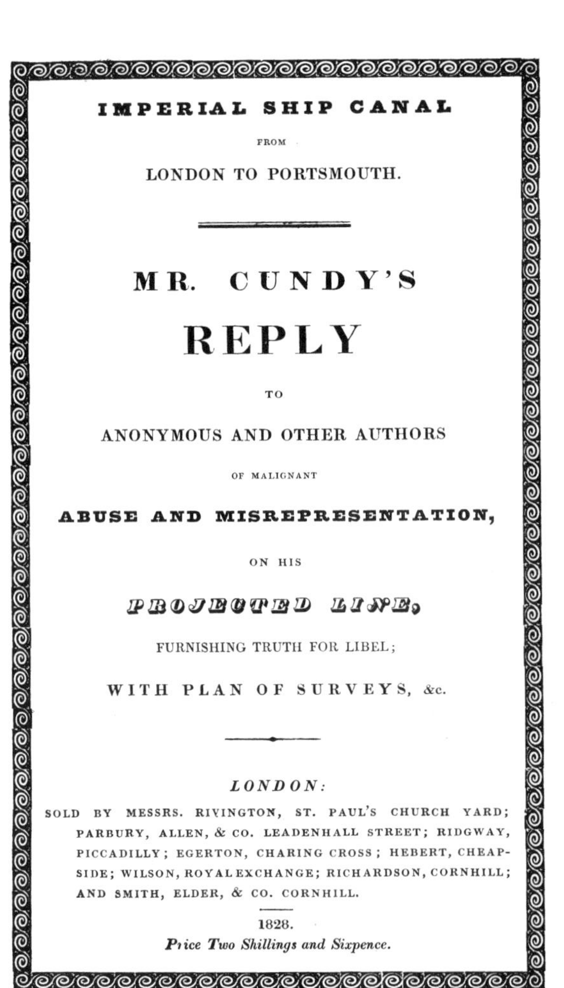
IMPERIAL SHIP CANAL

FROM

LONDON TO PORTSMOUTH.

MR. CUNDY'S

REPLY

TO

ANONYMOUS AND OTHER AUTHORS

OF MALIGNANT

ABUSE AND MISREPRESENTATION,

ON HIS

PROJECTED LINE,

FURNISHING TRUTH FOR LIBEL;

WITH PLAN OF SURVEYS, &c.

LONDON:

SOLD BY MESSRS. RIVINGTON, ST. PAUL'S CHURCH YARD; PARBURY, ALLEN, & CO. LEADENHALL STREET; RIDGWAY, PICCADILLY; EGERTON, CHARING CROSS; HEBERT, CHEAPSIDE; WILSON, ROYAL EXCHANGE; RICHARDSON, CORNHILL; AND SMITH, ELDER, & CO. CORNHILL.

1828.

Price Two Shillings and Sixpence.

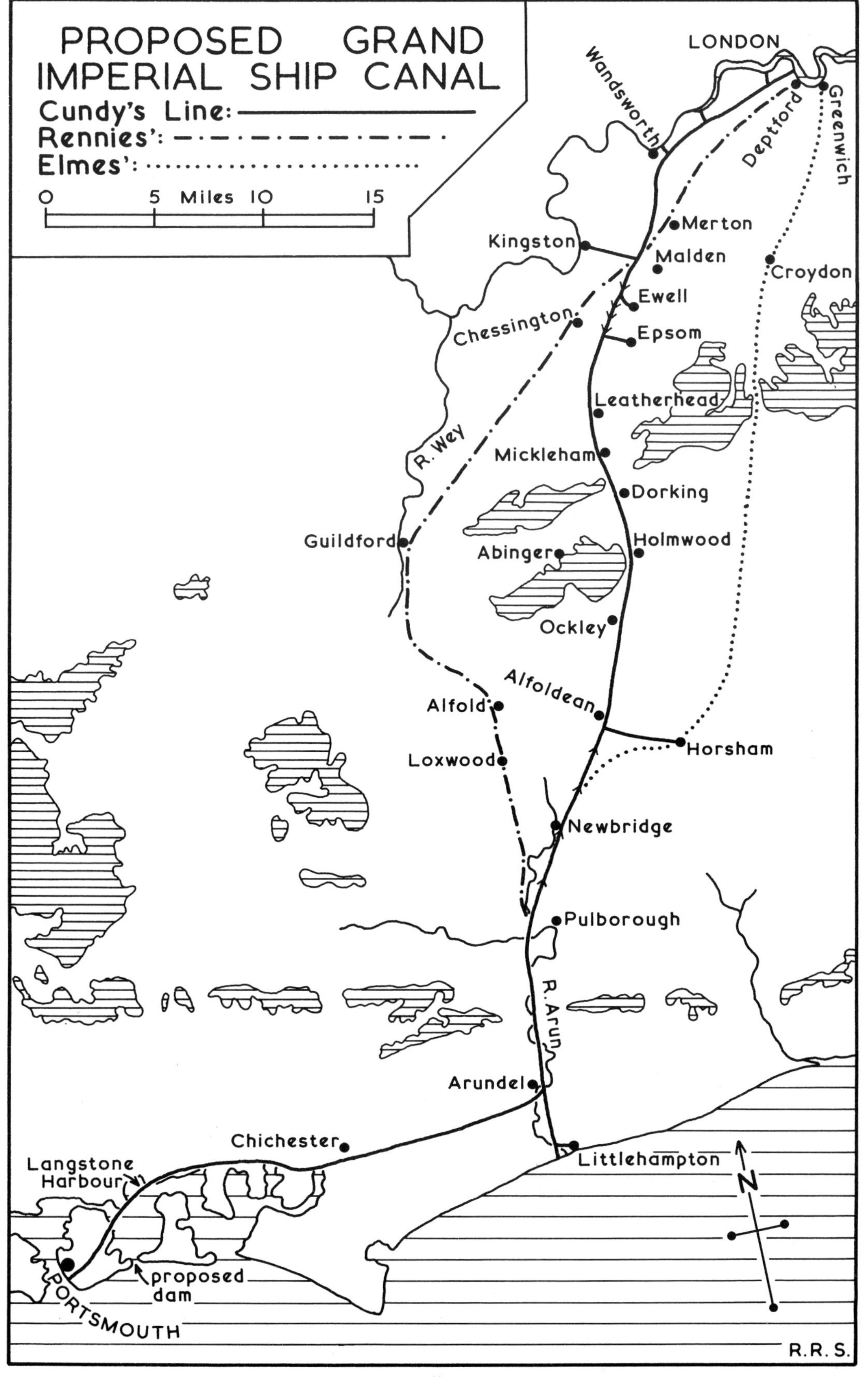
PROPOSED GRAND IMPERIAL SHIP CANAL
Cundy's Line:
Rennies':
Elmes':
0 5 Miles 10 15
LONDON
Wandsworth
Deptford
Greenwich
Merton
Kingston
Malden
Croydon
Ewell
Chessington
Epsom
Leatherhead
R. Wey
Mickleham
Dorking
Guildford
Abinger
Holmwood
Ockley
Alfoldean
Alfold
Horsham
Loxwood
Newbridge
Pulborough
R. Arun
Arundel
Chichester
Littlehampton
Langstone Harbour
N
proposed dam
PORTSMOUTH
R.R.S.

THE BASINGSTOKE CANAL

The Basingstoke Canal Act (1778) authorized a waterway nearly 44 miles long from the Wey Navigation at Woodham to Basingstoke by way of Woking, Frimley and Odiham with a branch to Turgis Green. The American War of Independence and that with France discouraged activity and it was not until 1787 that a prospectus of traffic and revenue was issued. At the same time it was decided to abandon the Turgis Green branch in favour of a 1230 yard long tunnel at Greywell which reduced the total length to 37 miles. William Jessop was appointed engineer and the canal was opened in 1794 at a cost of £153,000. As the original Act only authorized £126,000, a further Act (1793) increased this by £60,000. However the company had been paying interest on its bonds which accounted for £30,000 and although payments were suspended in 1796, the company never succeeded in developing enough traffic to pay off all the interest, let along a dividend. Tolls rarely exceeded £5000 pa, and seldom were more than 30,000 tons carried.

The chief cause of the navigation's lack of commercial success was the failure to extend the canal beyond Basingstoke in spite of an extraordinary number of attempts. For over thirty years proposals were made for linking the waterway with various towns, the English Channel and the Kennet & Avon Canal.

The London & Southampton Railway (opened in 1839) caused canal receipts to drop by about half but the construction of Aldershot Camp (1854–59) brought welcome traffic if only limited revenue. In 1866 the canal company went into voluntary liquidation and over the next fifty years the waterway fell into the hands of a succession of speculators, few more successful than the last. The purchase of the canal by A. J. Harmsworth in 1923 brought a revival in trade to Woking but when the gas company ceased to manufacture its own gas in 1936 a substantial proportion of the canal's remaining trade disappeared. Commercial traffic ended in 1949 and for many years the canal lay derelict, the locks unworkable and the bed in many places a marshy swamp, a habitat for migratory prams and broken bicycles.

The attempt to restore the waterway began with the formation of the Surrey & Hampshire Canal Society in 1966. By 1973 the society had 2000 members and was so successful in making known the potential amenity value of the old canal that both the Hampshire and Surrey County Councils were persuaded to obtain compulsory purchase orders in 1973 and 1976, so that restoration could be begun. Voluntary working parties and school-leavers, some employed by the Manpower Services Commission, have been working to clear the undergrowth, rebuild the locks and dredge the channel ever since. Both county councils and local companies have contributed handsomely in cash and in kind. Surrey has so far spent more than £800,000, Hampshire about £1 million. The introduction of a passenger boat service between Odiham and North Warnborough by the society in 1978 has been so successful that an average annual income of £10,500 was received between 1978 and 1983.

The latest news (September 1987) is that the canal will be reopened from Woodham to Greywell tunnel by the beginning of 1989. It is then hoped that work can start on reopening the tunnel (closed since 1932) and forming a new terminal basin at Up Nately. Restoration to Basingstoke is unlikely due to the advent of a motorway across the canal channel at Hatch between Basing and Mapledurwell.

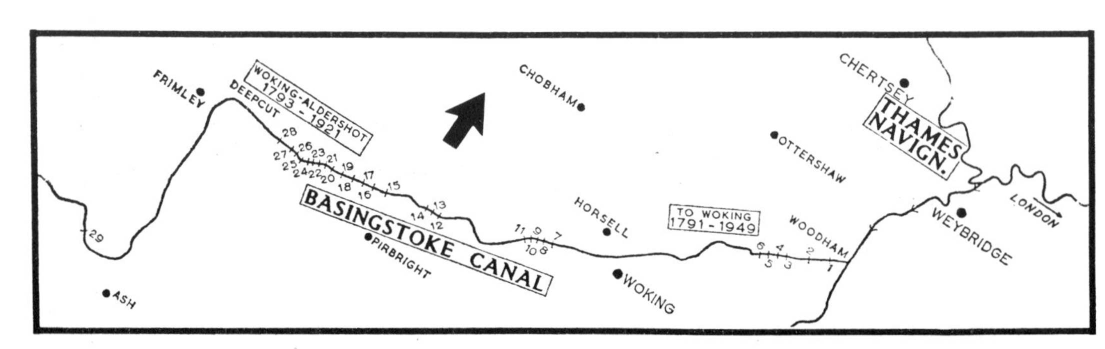

1. Entrance to the Basingstoke Canal at Woodham, Byfleet 1967.

2. Waiting to enter the first lock at Woodham 1967. The lock remained in disrepair from 1968 until its reopening this year (1987).

3. Woodham lock-house (1967) by Lock III, where tolls on all upgoing craft were collected. The stables (now demolished) were at the left side of the building.

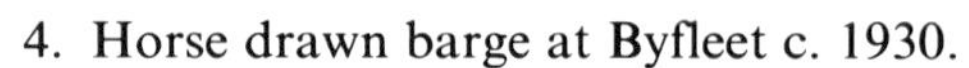

4. Horse drawn barge at Byfleet c. 1930.

5. Make-shift dry dock, now demolished, seen in 1966 erected above lock V at Woodham.

6. The Barge **Gwendoline** is pulled out of Scotland Lock, in the Woodham Flight in 1934, en route to Woking Gasworks loaded with 40 to 50 tons of coal. **Gwendoline** was built at Ash Vale in 1921 by A.J. Harmsworth, who used her for trading. She was sold in 1950.

7. Spanton's timber yard had a 240 yd frontage to the canal. This photograph was taken in 1967, five years before the wharf and buildings were demolished.

8. The last barge to unload timber here docked on 27th June 1949, but regular deliveries had ceased in 1947.

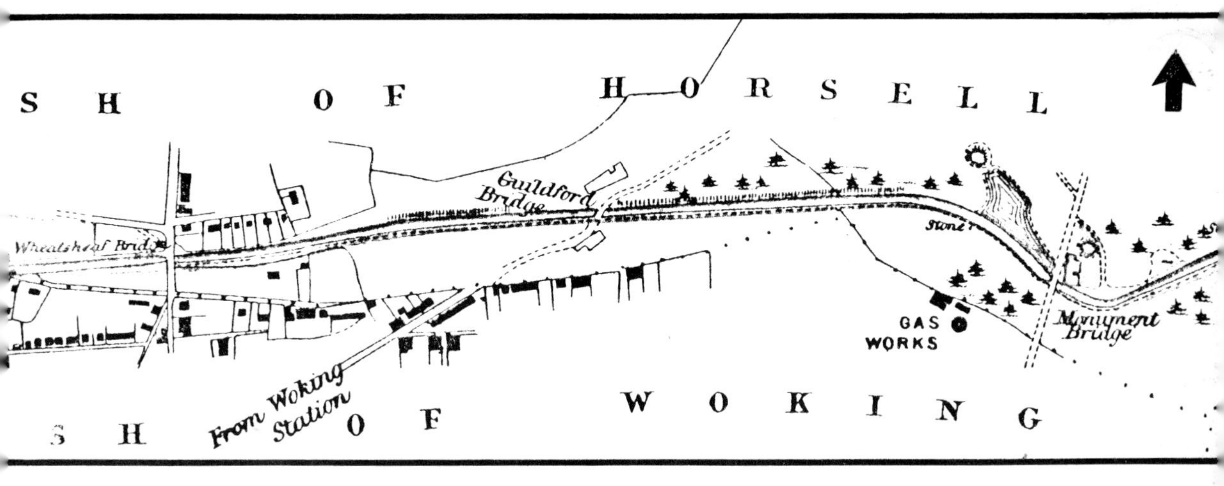

1904 map. Spanton's Wharf was situated above the M of Monument Bridge. Guildford Bridge now carries the A320.

9. The barge **Red Jacket** due to be unloaded at Spanton's Wharf in 1947. Most of the timber was loaded direct from ships discharging in the Surrey Docks. **Red Jacket** was built for A. J. Harmsworth at Berkhamstead in 1909. She was 72' 6" long, 13' 2" wide and could carry 70 tons of cargo.

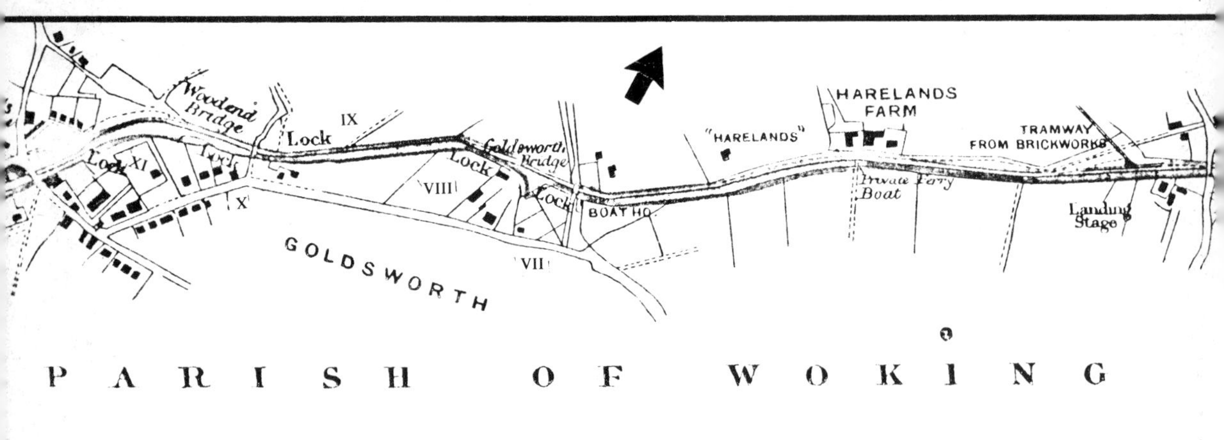

The 1904 map shows a tramway terminating at the canal side.

10. Abandoned barge at Woking between Harelands Farm and Arthur's Bridge in 1967.

→

11. Workmen preparing to begin work on cleaning the channel in the Goldsworth flight of locks at Woking in 1913. Lock IX in background with both paddles drawn. The unusual white lock gates were the result of an accidental spillage of paint on part of the gate whilst under construction which necessitated painting both gates white!

12. This shows the labourers at work cleaning out the reach.

13. Lock XII, Brookwood in 1966
The concrete pill box erected as an anti-invasion measure in 1940 was demolished by Surrey County Council in 1987 to enable the balance beams of the lock to be replaced.

14. The pound approaching Lock XIII in 1987, after the lock had been restored.

15. Locks XIII and XIV at Brookwood in 1967.

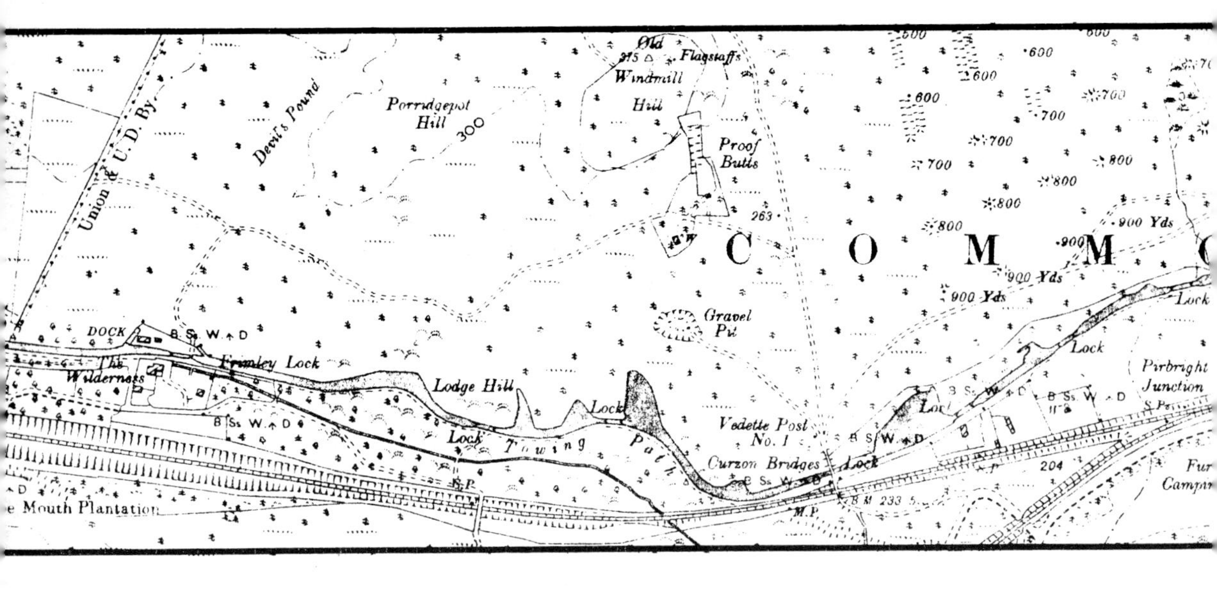

16. Local authorities had great difficulty in establishing who was responsible for maintaining bridges over the canal after the original company had gone into voluntary liquidation. After Woking Urban District Council failed to win its case against the London & South-Western Canal Company (alias the Basingstoke Canal) in 1913, the local councils went ahead and erected new bridges themselves. The plaque reads "Pirbright Bridge 1915 erected by the Guildford Rural District Council on the site of a brick bridge formerly owned by the Basingstoke and Aldershot Canal Company."

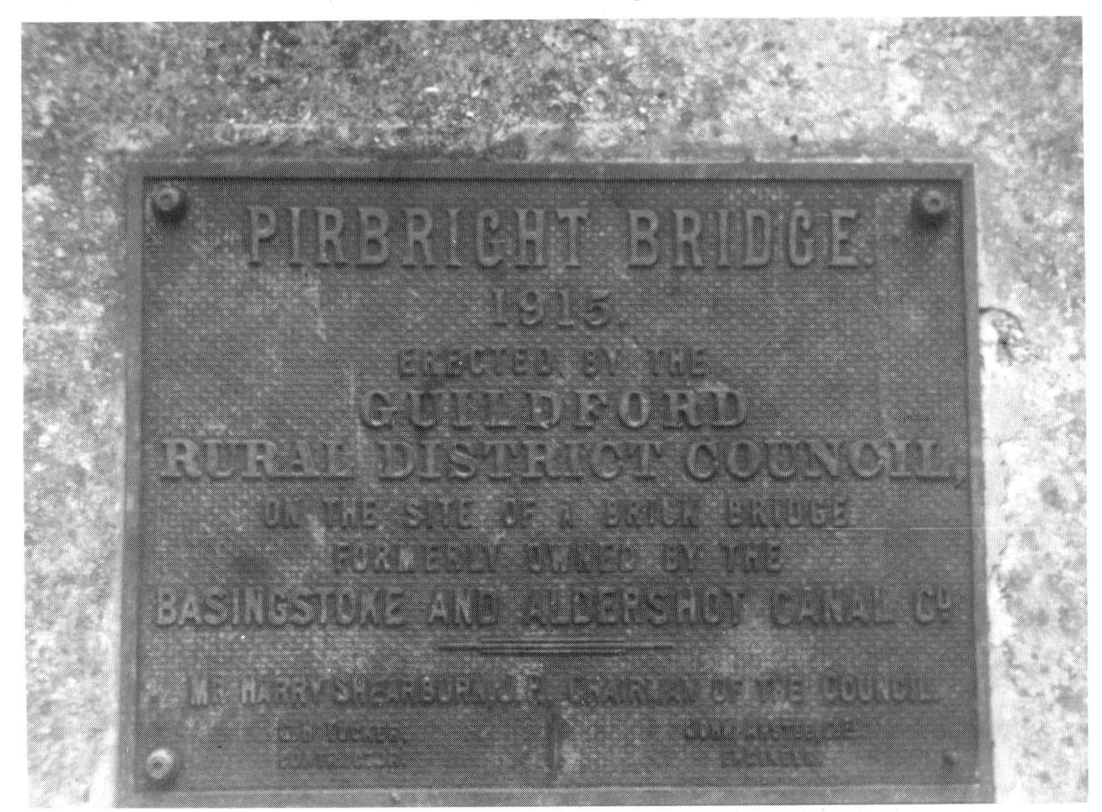

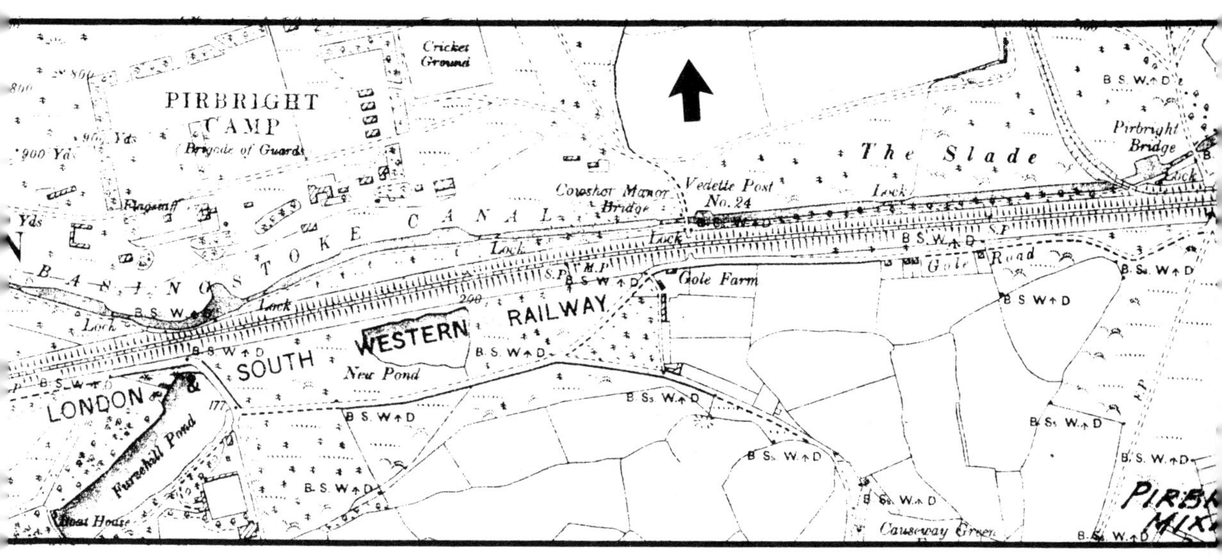

1870 survey of 6" to 1 mile of Frimley Locks. 13 locks between Pirbright Wharf and Frimley Dock raised the water level 97½ feet. This section of the canal, last used for regular commercial traffic in 1921 had become unusable by the end of WW2. It was reopened amidst much rejoining in 1985.

17. Skeleton of a steel narrow boat at Pirbright Wharf (1968) and Lock XV. Pirbright Bridge can be seen behind the lock-gates. The boat was one of a pair **Maudie** and **Ada,** believed to have been purchased by a family from Richmond (Surrey) from the Nateley Brickworks about 1906. The new owner with his family aboard, had the boat bow-hauled down the canal but the trip had to be abandoned when the family contracted diphtheria.

19. When the London & Southampton Railway Act (1837) was passed, it included clauses to protect the canal company. Section XXII forced the railway to build a wall sufficiently high to prevent the barge horses from being frightened by the locomotives where the line was within 100 feet of the canal. When Freeling's railway companion was published in 1839, the author commented that 'the directors were compelled to build a turf wall of considerable extent (Section XXI), under the pretence that their trains would frighten the Rozinantes which draw the canal barges, although they had been accustomed for months to see trains of ballast wagons running backwards and forwards many more times in the day than the trains; if this were opposition or intended to annoy the company or to retard the opening of the line, how dignified was the opposition!' How bold the effort! What ingenuity in the mind that suggested the idea! In September 1880 the canal overflowed washing down part of the wall on to the track and subsequently damaging an engine and sixteen wagons. This view shows the wall in 1968 below Cowshot Manor Bridge.

18. Pirbright Wharf Cottage and Lock XV 1954. The London and Southampton Railway line can be seen on the high embankment in the background. The Act (1837) stipulated that where the railway was 25 feet above the tow-path and within 100 feet of the canal a close furze hedge had to be planted on a four high bank to prevent barge horses being frightened by the engines. There is no sign of the hedge in this view.

20. Lock XVII (1966). Cowshot Bridge in foreground. The lock was re-opened in 1982.

21. The Brigade of Guards Swimming Pool (1966), last used about 1954, was situated two locks below Hodgebottom Bridge between Locks XXII and XXIII. This view is taken from Lock XXII showing how the pool was built between the canal banks. J. R. Colville, Sir Winston Churchill's private secretary, recalls in his biography of Field Marshall Lord Gort V.C. that when Gort was an ensign in the Grenadier Guards (1905–7) he was far from popular during his early years in the regiment. "Honest, good-humoured and imperturbable though he might be, there were occasions when his brother officers thought his devotion to duty went altogether too far, and on one occasion they threw him into the Basingstoke Canal at Pirbright for taking life too seriously".

22. Frimley Lock XXVI in 1968. Restoration of the flight of 14 locks took five years and could not have been so quickly completed without help from the Manpower Services Commission's training schemes which granted the Surrey & Hampshire Canal Society more than £½ million between 1977 and 1983.

23. Frimley Lock XXVIII in 1987 in fully restored working order.

BASINGSTOKE
CANAL
NAVIGATION.

TAKE NOTICE,

That all Persons Trespassing on these PLANTATIONS under any pretence whatever, or committing *Damage, Injury,* or *Spoil thereon, will be* forthwith prosecuted.

By Order of the Company of Proprietors of the Basingstoke Canal Navigation.

CHARLES HEADEACH,
Clerk to the Company.

Basingstoke, 1st October, 1858.

R. Cottle, Printer, Basingstoke.

24. Frimley – 1858 and 1987 – The warning notices seem to be more in evidence than they were during the nineteenth century.

25. Pleasure steamer moored by the carpenter's shop and forge at Frimley Lock XXVIII c. 1890. The dock lies just beyond the steamer. The steam launch was probably the *Una* owned by Peter Willans who was a well known engineer and inventor of the central valve steam engine used in early power stations before the steam turbine era. The *Una*, 70 feet long and 7' 3" broad, was moored regularly at Frimley and had stanchions around the deck to restrain the young Willans family from falling overboard. Peter Willans was killed in an accident in 1892. His son Kyrle Willans, also a mechanical engineer, introduced Tom Rolt to engineering and canals in the 1920's. The Una subsequently went to the Norfolk Broads before 1900.

A.J. HARMSWORTH & SONS
ALDERSHOT.

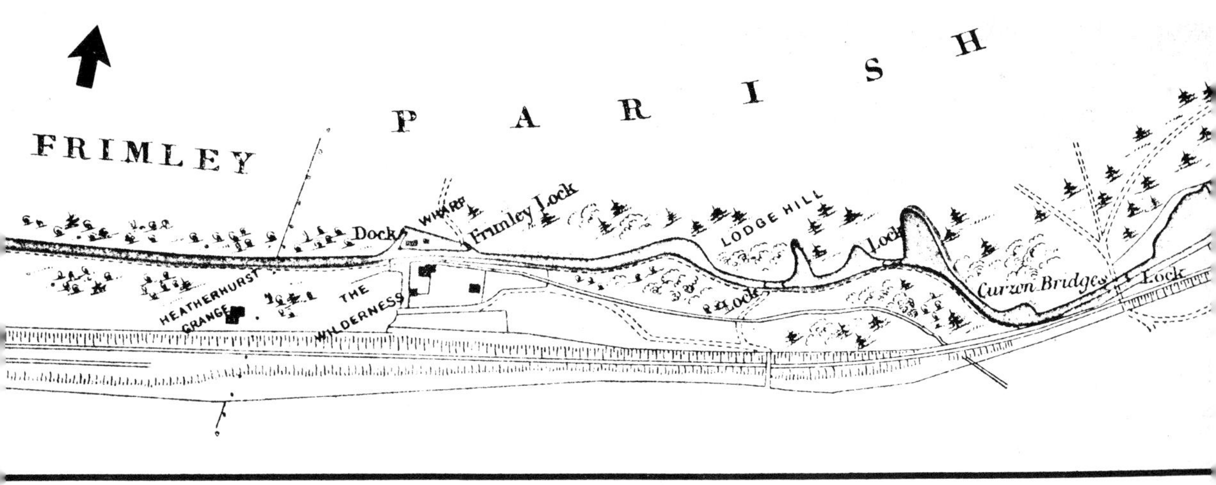

1904 map. The screen wall was between the canal and the railway, west of Curzon Bridges.

←

26. The reclaimed dock at Frimley (1987). After being unused since 1912 it was filled in during 1939, but was restored and reopened by the Surrey & Hampshire Canal Society in 1984.

29. A post card depicting Deepcut Bridge, Frimley Green (c. 1910). The bridge was rebuilt after WW2. The deep cutting through Frimley Hill gave its name to the area. Deepcut remains a thousand yard cutting seventy feet deep in places.

←

28. German prisoners of war unloading timber from **Dauntless** at Frimley Wharf in 1916.

30.31. The aqueduct over the London to Southampton Railway at Frimley Green in 1968. It was originally built with two arches in 1838 but was extended to four when the railway track was widened in 1902.

32. In 1897 the London & South Western Railway obtained parliamentary powers to provide quadruple track to Basingstoke which entailed rebuilding the twin arched aqueduct over the railway at Frimley. The work was carried out in 1902 and, so as to avoid detaining commercial water traffic for which the railway company would have been liable for heavy damages, it was decided to rebuild the aqueduct twice the necessary width so that the flow of barge traffic would not be interrupted while work proceeded.

33. The same scene in 1984. King's Head Bridge carrying the road from Frimley Green to Brookwood is in the background.

34. A view of Frimley Green, looking towards the aqueduct, circa. 1910. The boathouse was built at about that time and provided skiffs for hire until WW2.

35. Taken in 1965 from the same view point as the previous photograph, the partially closed stop gates are visible. These, together with a similar pair on the far side of the aqueduct were provided as a safety precaution in 1940. They could have been closed to prevent the railway being flooded, in the event of the aqueduct being breached by enemy action.

37. Mytchett Lake is rather surprisingly omitted from the 1790 plan of the canal by William Wright of Frimley although other lakes are shown. It is therefore assumed that both Great Bottom Flash and Mytchett Lake were natural hollows which were formed into reservoirs when the canal was built.

36. Close up view of a stop gate in 1976.

38. Derelict reminders of the canal's commercial days. The hulks of narrow boats **Basingstoke, Greywell** and **Mapledurwell** lying in Great Bottom Flash, Ash Vale in 1954 together with an old punt, the **Mudlark,** used for dredging and ice-breaking; at left can be seen the float of a former sea-plane used during WW2. The **Basingstoke** had been

licenced in the 1880's and was laid up in 1933. The other narrow boats built in 1912 were used to carry flour from Weybridge to Aldershot, timber from Crookham to London and military stores during WW1. When WW2 broke out they were moored in the flash as anti-invasion obstacles. (see also photograph no. 72)

39. Barge building began at Ash Vale in 1918. On average one boat a year was laid down until 1935. All barges were built of oak, 72' 6" long, 13' $10\frac{1}{2}$" wide with $2\frac{1}{2}$ inch thick Columbian pine bottoms. This view shows the **Brookwood** being built in 1930. When commercial traffic ceased the **Brookwood**, which could carry 75 tons, was turned into a houseboat and for some years was moored on the River Thames near Reading.

40. The refloating of the **Perseverance** at Ash Vale in 1947, after a refit. *The* **Perseverance** had been originally built in 1922.

41. P.A.L. Vine, a vice-president of the Surrey & Hampshire Canal Society driving a golden nail into the first new lock gate to be built by members of the society. The ceremony took place at the former barge repairing yard at Ash Vale in 1969. The gate – one of a pair of lower gates – was later fitted in Ash Lock with a pair of upper gates, also built by volunteers. Cranley Onslow, MP for Woking and president of the Society stands, hands behind back, while Tony Harmsworth looks on.

42. The Ash Vale Boat House c. 1968. The large corrugated iron shed was used for building barges by Alec Harmsworth, the canal's owner from 1925 until 1947. 15 barges 72' 6" long x 13' 10½" wide able to carry up to 80 tons were built between 1918 and 1935. Repairs were carried out on the opposite bank until 1947, when **Perseverance** was the last boat to be refloated there.

43. The frozen canal at Ash Vale during the arctic weather of 1947 serves as a reminder of the days and sometimes weeks, when ice prevented barges being able to move. When the ice was more than half an inch thick, ice breakers had to be used or trade was brought to a standstill. In the 1920's the dredging punt *Mudlark* was used for this purpose. Ash Vale boathouse can be seen to the left of the railway bridge.

44. Ash Vale Wharf c. 1915 was a busy trading centre until 1921. It also remained a popular pleasure boating station catered for by Knowles boathouse until 1949.

45. Pleasure boating in 1915 along the 1000 yard long Ash Vale embankment. In mid-reach, the canal crosses the county boundary formed by the River Blackwater and enters Hampshire. After commercial traffic ceased to Aldershot in 1920, it remained barely navigable due to weeds and silt. The breach of the embankment during the great floods of 1968 drained this section and threatened the future of the canal. However a major recovery operation by the Surrey & Hampshire Canal Society who laid down a railway along the embankment restored this part of the navigation in 1984. 14000 tons of clay were needed to repuddle the water channel.

CROYDON CANAL

The Croydon Canal stretched $9\frac{1}{4}$ miles from the Grand Surrey Canal at New Cross to Croydon. It was built by Dudley Clarke to take 30 to 35 ton barges. 26 locks made to take craft 60ft x 9ft raised the water level 167 feet in the $2\frac{1}{2}$ mile ascent of Forest Hill from whence there was a $5\frac{1}{2}$ mile level reach to Selhurst before two more locks brought the waterway to the terminal basin on the site of what is now West Croydon Station. It had been hoped to extend the canal to Portsmouth. John Rennie's scheme of 1803 envisaged a 100 mile long canal with 41 locks and a 4400 yard tunnel at Merstham. William Jessop on the other hand proposed extending the Surrey Iron railway but neither project received sufficient financial support.

The canal's main traffic was carrying coal, manure and general merchandise to Croydon and bringing back agricultural produce, fuller's earth, lime, stone and timber to the Thames. Its commercial success was limited by the competition it suffered from the Surrey Iron Railway which had been opened in 1803 from the Thames at Wandsworth to Croydon and extended to Merstham in 1805. The canal company built a 700 yard tramway from its terminus to Croydon Station which carried much of the traffic brought by rail from the Merstham quarries.

The canal and the iron railway competed against each other for some twenty five years with little evidence to show that mules or donkeys pulling trucks were any more profitable than horses pulling boats. Neither company paid a dividend of more than one per cent. In 1834 Joseph Gibbs recommended that a new railway line to Croydon should make use of the bed of the canal as a result of which the railway company, after much negotiation, bought the waterway for £40,250. The canal was closed in August 1836 and West Croydon Station was built on the site of the terminal basin and adjacent warehouses.

A century and a half later, there is little in evidence to point to its former existence. A lake used as a reservoir in South Norwood; a retaining wall forming part of the old Gloucester Road canal bridge in Croydon; curving streets which follow the former channel of the navigation (such as Albert Road, Elden Park and Lincoln Road in South Norwood), and a stretch of canal which has been preserved as an ornamental pond in Betts Park, near Anerley station. These are all that remain.

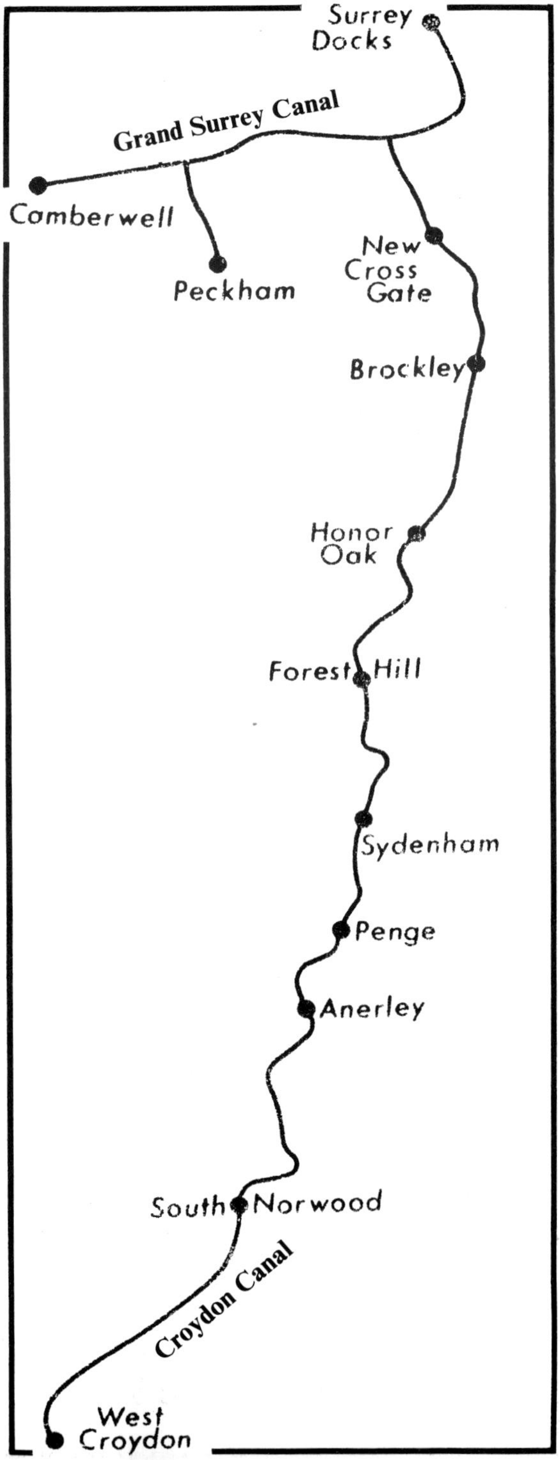

46. A view of the canal (1815) looking towards Deptford from the lock-keeper's house and showing a barge heading south and approaching the last lock (no. 28) before the level stretch to Croydon.

SHARE No. 2303.

THIS IS TO CERTIFY, that *George Grote of Threadneedle Street London Esquire* ——————

is the Proprietor of the share numbered as above, and is so entered in the Register of the said Company, and is entitled to the proportionate Profits and Advantages arising from the Undertaking.

GIVEN under the Common Seal of the said Company,

the *14th* ——— Day of *June* ——— 1817.

47. Sydenham Bridge c. 1820. This view from the tow-path looking north by an unknown artist, shows a barge with an unusually low roofed cabin. A man can be seen standing on the prow of a second barge moored beyond the bridge. A triangular slatted coop reveals a chicken's head at right. The house is on the site of the first railway station at Sydenham opened in June 1839.

The lock-keeper's cottage at Brockley c. 1910. The building stood in Shardeloes Road (formerly part of the canal bed) until it was demolished in 1946.

48. A cut-off section of the derelict canal from one of a series of 1854 views of the Crystal Palace. Anerley Railway Station opened in 1839 at left.

49. This ornamental stretch of water in Betts Park, Anerley is the only part of the canal bed extant in 1987.

THE GODALMING NAVIGATION

The Wey Navigation Act (1760) extended the waterway $4\frac{1}{2}$ miles from Guildford to Godalming. Four locks were built and an extensive wharf was developed at Godalming. During the American War of Independence considerable amounts of government stores were brought down from London to Godalming by water and carried from there by land to Portsmouth. Another important item was the carriage of gun-powder brought by waggon from the Chilworth powder mills to Stonebridge Wharf, Shalford. After the closure of the mills in 1921, only two barges reguarly worked the river between the two world wars. Godalming Wharf ceased to be used in 1925, commercial traffic above Guildford ceased in 1950 and in 1969 the navigation was handed over to the National Trust. It is now regularly used by pleasure craft.

50. Guildford Town Bridge in the 1860's. The original five arch stone bridge had to be altered when the navigation was extended to Godalming in 1763. The alteration attracted unfavourable comment. One writer referred to it in 1828 as 'one of the clumsiest pieces of architecture that ever disgraced a civilized place of residence' and went on to remark that the widening of the bridge with iron arches in 1825, as depicted here, had produced a 'graceful and durable structure'. However during the great floods in February 1900 timber from Moon's yard blocked the arches and caused the bridge to collapse.

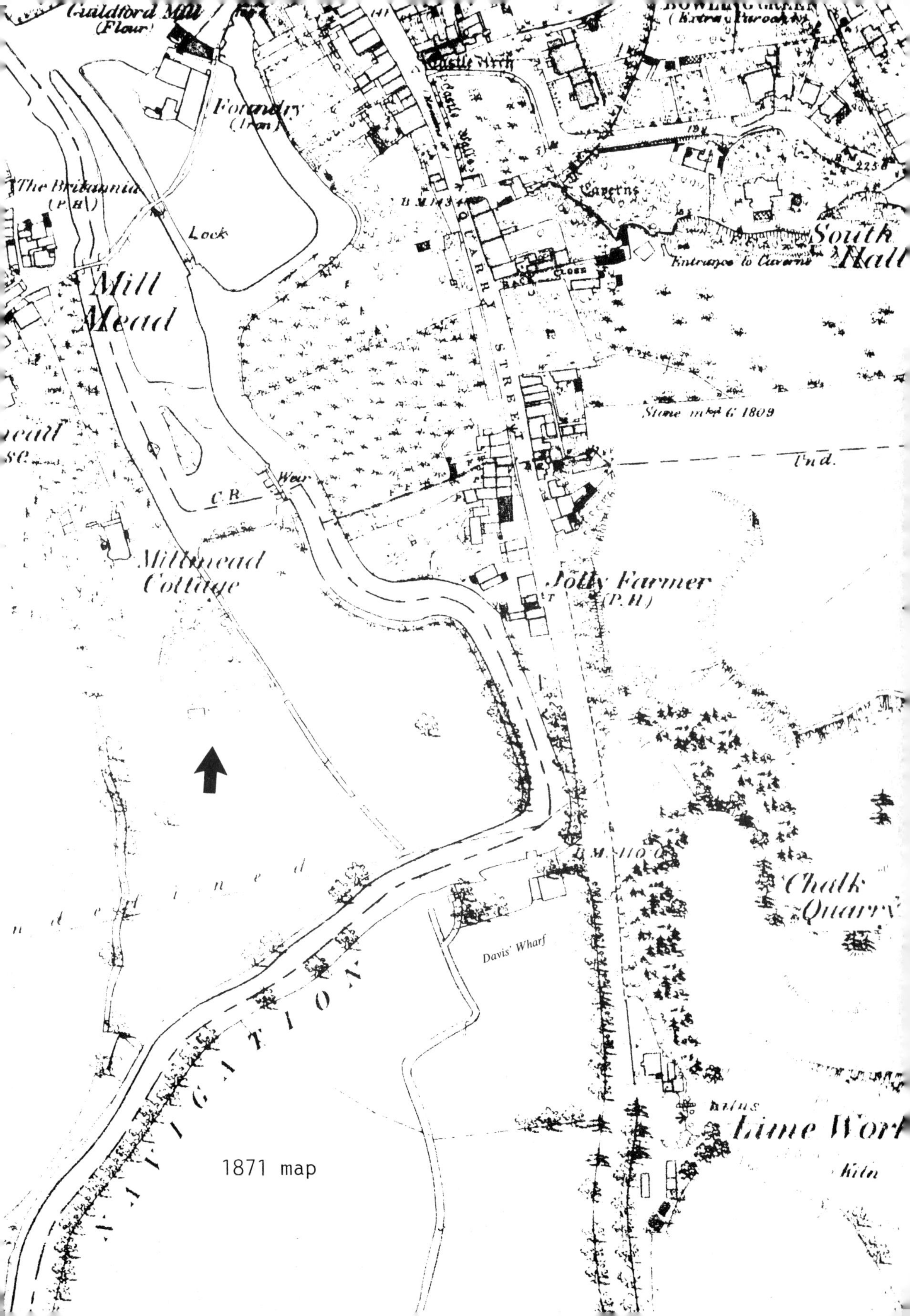

Guildford Mill (Flour)

Foundry (Iron)

Castle Arch

Castle Walls

Bowling Green (Extra Parochial)

The Britannia (P.H.)

Lock

Mill Mead

Caverns

South Hall

Entrance to Caverns

Quarry Street

Back Close

Stone mkd G 1809

Weir

C.R.

Millmead Cottage

Jolly Farmer (P.H.)

Chalk Quarry

Davis' Wharf

Navigation

Kilns

Lime Works

Kiln

1871 map

51. A print showing sailing barges above Guildford Bridge c. 1790. Guildford Castle in the background.

52. Unloading grain at Guildford Flour Mill, 1881. The mill operated from 1771 to 1894. The mill now houses the props of the adjacent Yvonne Arnaud Theatre, opened in 1965.

53. The popularity of pleasure boating increased tenfold between 1870 and 1890. Leroy's boathouse (c. 1900) flourished for many years and the name is now perpetuated by Guildford Boat House's cruising restaurant Alfred Leroy.

THE

COMMISSIONERS

FOR extending the Navigation of the River *Wey*, from *Guildford* to *Godalming* in *Surrey*, do hereby give Notice, that the ſaid River is now open and navigable; and that they have this Day, at their Meeting, ſettled the following Rates and Duties upon all Goods to be navigated on the ſame, *viz.*

From the Wharf at *Godalming* to *Guildford.*

	£.	s.	d.
For all Timber and dry Goods *per* Load, — — —	0	1	5
For Coals *per* Chaldron, — — — —	0	1	3
For Chalk *per* Load, — — — — —	0	0	6
For Woollen Rags and other Kinds of Manure, — — —	0	0	9

From *Stone Bridge Brook* Wharf.

	£.	s.	d.
For all Timber and dry Goods *per* Load, — — — —	0	1	2
For Coals *per* Chaldron, — — — — — —	0	1	0
For Chalk *per* Load, — — — — —	0	0	4
For Woollen Rags and other Kinds of Manure, — — —	0	0	6

AND the Barge Maſters, having undertaken to carry Goods at nine Pence *per* Load Freightage, from *Godalming* Wharf to *Guildford*; and from *Stone Bridge Brook* Wharf to *Guildford* at ſix Pence *per* Load; this added to the reſpective Tolls above-mentioned, include all Charges of Carriage from the reſpective Wharfs.

May 29th, 1764.

Guildford: Printed by CHARLES MARTIN, at the *Angel* and *Bible* in *High-ſtreet*, M.DCC.LXIV.

54. Loading chalk from the immense Guildford Quarry into George Davis' barge at Davis' wharf c. 1870. John Davis had leased two chalk pits at the quarry from the Wey & Arun Junction Canal Company since 1821.

55. There were only 4 locks on the navigation. Tolls were collected at the second lock up, St. Catherine's whose cottage (seen here c. 1908) was situated 400 yards above the lock and ½ mile from Stonebridge Wharf where the navigation was joined by the Wey & Arun Junction Canal.

5. This wooden railway viaduct was built y the Reading, Guildford & Reigate railway ompany over the navigation between St. atherine's Lock and Broadford Bridge, halford in 1849. The barge is proceeding owards Guildford. The viaduct was replaced 1912.

7. Loading gunpowder at Stonebridge Vharf c. 1900. The red flag is flying from e barge. The powder was brought by horse rawn waggon from the Chilworth Mills. In ugust 1864 a newly delivered barge – the st to be built at the Pallingham boatyard belonging to Samuel Sharpe of Chilworth, d been loaded with gunpowder at onebridge wharf, and was only a mile or from the wharf when it exploded. The vo men on board were blown to pieces and e vessel sank. These dangerous cargoes ontinued to be carried by water to the agazines at Woolwich, Purfleet, and arking Creek until 1921.

RIVER WEY from *Godalming* to *Guildford.*
Godalming Commissioners Account from the 25 Day of December 1766 to the 25 Day of March following.

Places of Loading and Unloading and Prices of Riverage.	No. of Loads.	at *per* Load.	£.	S.	D.
		S. D.			
GODALMING - -	115	1 5	8	2	11
Stone Bridge - - -	- -	1 2	- -	- -	-
Coals to GODALMING	29	1 3	1	16	3
Rags to Ditto - -	- -	0 9	- -	- -	-
			9	19	2

58. This must be one of the least illuminating views of Godalming (c. 1908) ever printed since it is taken $1\frac{1}{2}$ miles from Godalming Wharf and of the town not even the church spire is visible. What it does show is that punting was in vogue on this section of the waterway.

The 1870 map of Godalming Wharf shows no trace of the dock filled in in 1832 nor of the swing bridge but the gasworks were established near the wharf before the railway reached the town in 1849. Although the wharf was fully operational in 1870 no names of buildings are given on the map. This 1895 survey shows that the lay-out of the wharf had hardly changed. Commercial traffic ceased in 1925 but it was not until after WW2 that the area was razed and redeveloped.

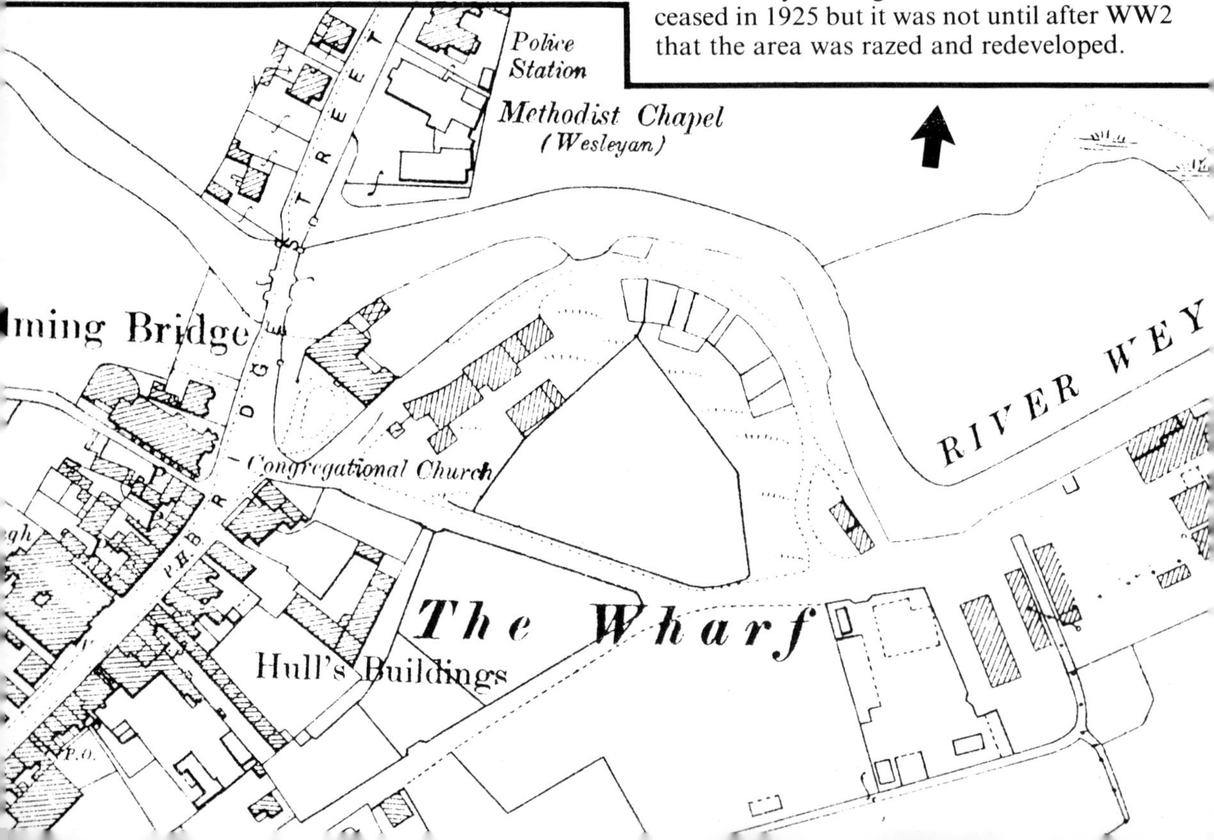

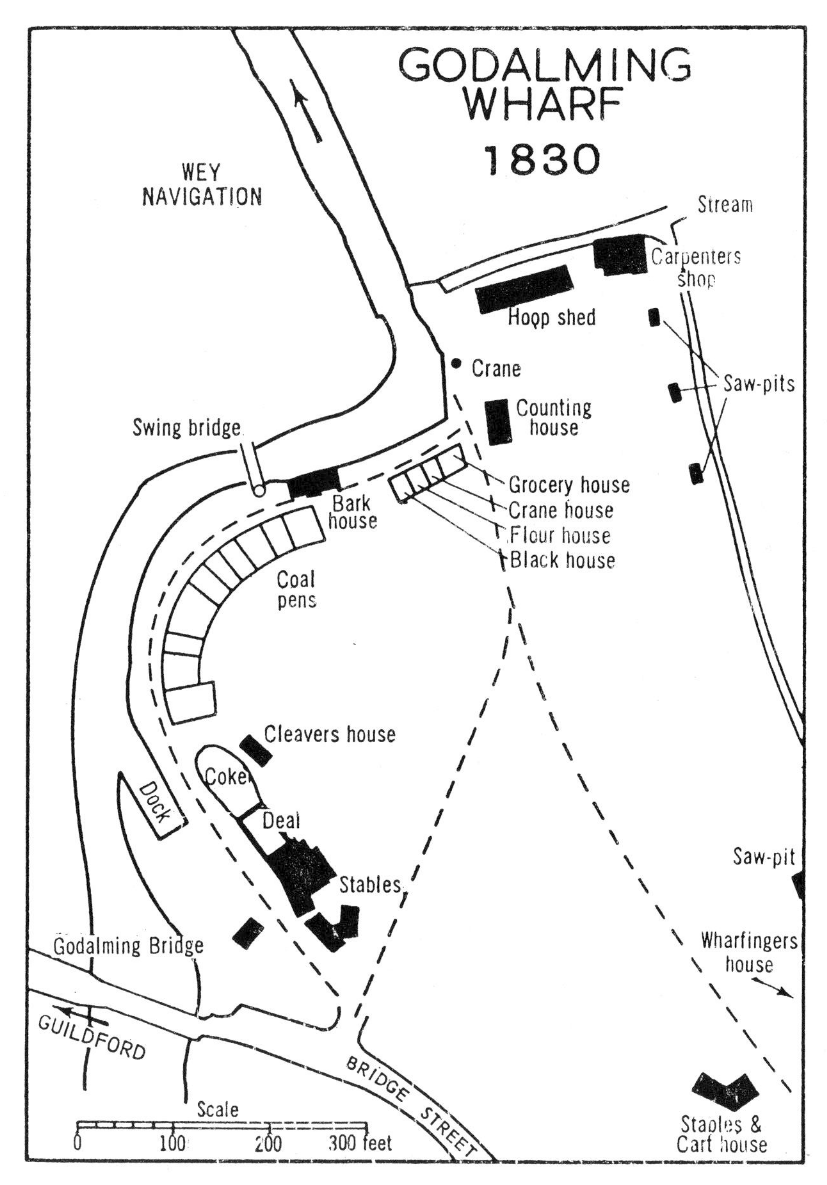

1830 plan.

GODALMING NAVIGATION.

WANTED, a WHARFINGER, to reside at the Godalming Wharf. Wages 17s. per week, with house rent free. No one need apply who has not some knowledge of the duties of a Wharfinger, and can keep clear and accurate accounts; and he must have an unexceptionable character.

Applications in writing, enclosing testimonials, to be sent to the clerk, Mr. H. Stedman, Godalming, on or before Monday, the 23rd inst.

THE GRAND SURREY CANAL

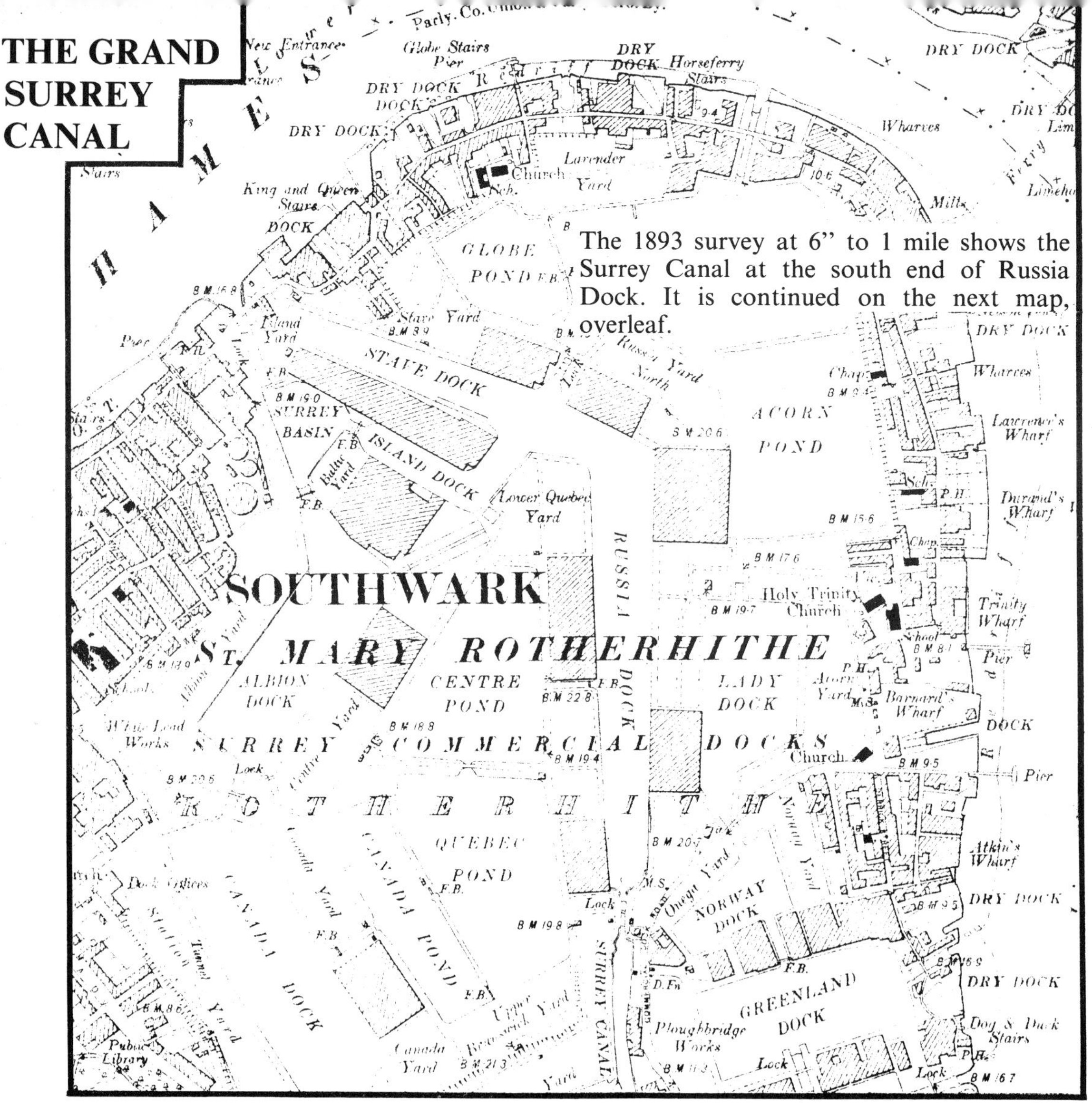

The 1893 survey at 6” to 1 mile shows the Surrey Canal at the south end of Russia Dock. It is continued on the next map, overleaf.

The Grand Surrey Canal was built between 1801 and 1810 from the Thames at Rotherhithe to Camberwell, a distance of just over 3 miles. Originally it had been intended to reach Mitcham but in 1803 the company decided to develop dock facilities by building a ship lock and widening the canal to form the 3 acre Grand Surrey Basin which was opened in 1807. In 1826 an 1100 yard branch to Peckham was completed but the intended cut to the Borough and the Thames at Vauxhall were never begun. However in 1809 the Grand Surrey Canal had been joined at New Cross by the Croydon Canal which itself was closed in 1836.

In 1855 the Company became the Grand Surrey Docks & Canal Comany which nine years later amalgamated with the Commercial Docks Company to control and develop the Surrey docks complex. The Albion Dock Canada Dock (16 acres) was opened in 1876 with four grain warehouses, each with a capacity of 35000 tons, and 23 sheds, covering 46 acres, for storing timber. In 1904 the extension of Greenland Docks absorbed that section of the canal. The Port of London Authority assumed control of the Surrey Commercial Docks in 1908 which by then covered 372 acres.

1945 and the end of the Second World War saw the last barge load delivered to a canalside factory in Camberwell and the basin in disuse. In 1960 the western section was drained and as ships docked further downstream only the timber trade enabled the Surrey Docks to remain open until 1970. The 72 acre section of the Surrey Canal was last used in March 1971. The docks and the canal were filled in to form a strip of recreational land in the latter half of the 1970’s.

59. An aerial view (c. 1935) of the canal where it had been integrated into the enlarged Greenland Dock reopened in 1904 (foreground) and the Canada Dock (opened in 1876), St. Paul's Cathedral can be seen behind Tower Bridge.

60. The Grand Surrey Canal was lined with timber wharves since timber from Scandinavia and North America formed the principal traffic of the Surrey Docks.

The point where the Croydon Canal left the Grand Surrey Canal can be seen in the short arm between the 'Pepper Mill' and the D of **DEPTFORD.** Coldblow Pepper Mill was only erected in the 1880's and the development of Archangel Wharf and its dock basins adjacent to this arm had yet to be begun. This section of the Croydon Canal was filled in during the late 1960's, Archangel Wharf in 1972 and the whole area cleared for redevelopment in 1985. Although the Croydon Canal was closed in 1836, the London & Croydon railway used this arm as a canal-railway interchange until the Depford Wharf railway was opened in 1849.

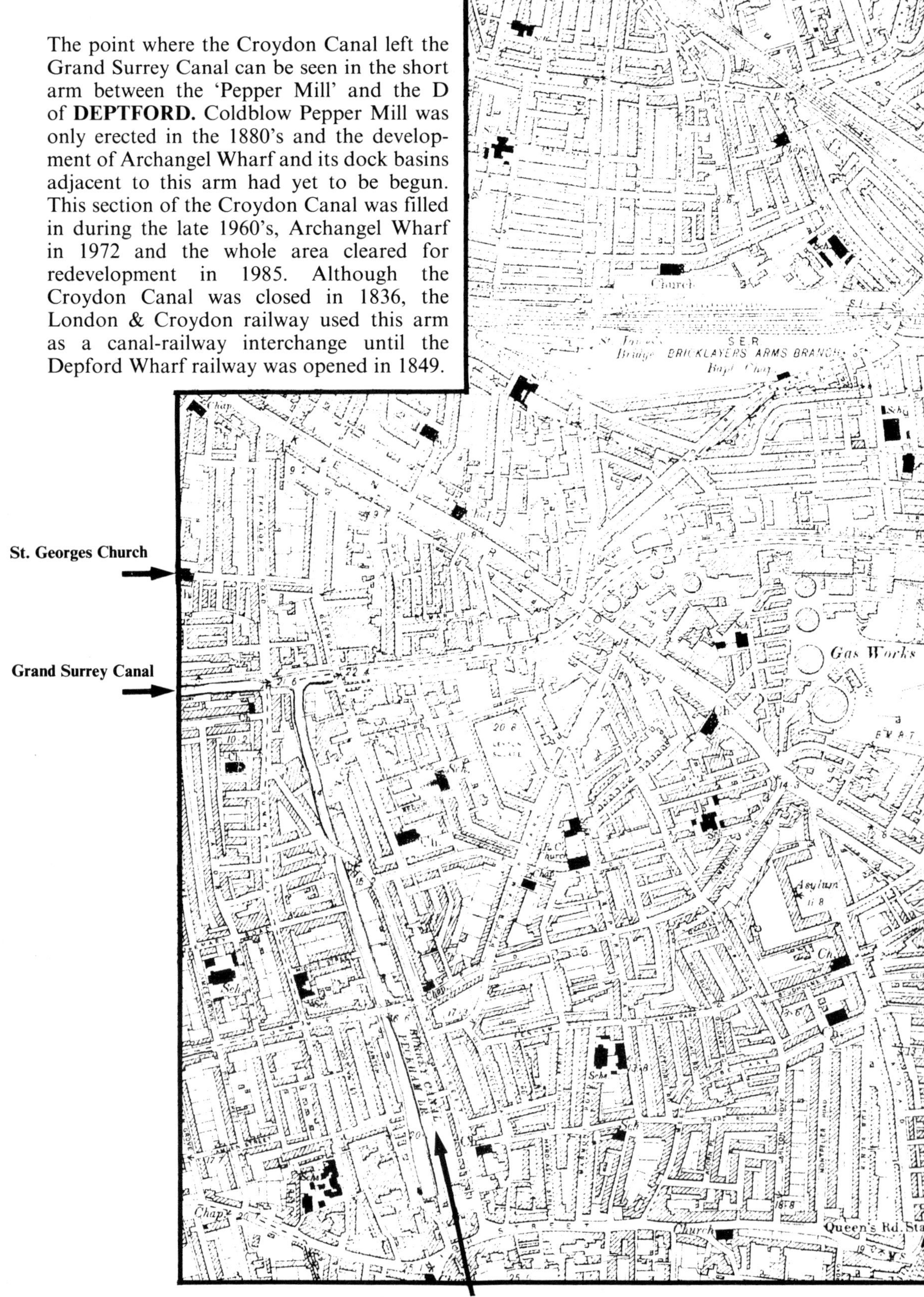

The Oval
(Cricket Ground)
Deptford Rd Station
SOUTH DOCK
WET DOCK
India Rubber Works
Bermondsey
Mission Ch
Torr's Works
Tramway Depot
EAST LONDON RAILWAY
LONDON & GREENWICH RY
S.E.R.
BRICKLAYERS ARMS BR
SOUTH BERMONDSEY SPUR
SOUTH LONDON LINE
L.B.& S.C.R.
SURREY
CANAL
Pepper Mill
DEPTFORD
Mission Church
Gas Works
Coldblow Crossing
Coldblow Farm
L.B.& S.C.R.
OLD KENT ROAD SPUR
School
Old Kent Road Sta
New Cross Sta
Aske's Hatcham School
St. James's Church

61. Looking east towards Deptford from the old Kent Road, c. 1920. The South Metropolitan Gas Light & Coke Company acquired their first site here in 1832 and produced gas until 1953. The gasholders can still be seen.

62. 'Unloading timber' – a painting by R. S. Reeve dated 1920 showing St. George's church, Camberwell in the background.

63. The sailing barge 'Ivy' moored below St. Georges Bridge, Camberwell in 1925.

64. Although the canal has been filled in two road bridges over the Peckham branch have been spared from demolition. Commercial Road Bridge, seen in 1987, with its ornate iron ballustrading was built in 1870.

65 The terminus of the Peckham Branch c. 1930, Peckham High Street is behind the crane. The basin was 450 feet by 80 feet. The branch has now been filled in and grassed over but two Victorian road bridges and a milepost have been retained.

Milepost, the only surviving post in situ in Surrey, on the former tow-path by Taylor's Bridge, $3\frac{1}{2}$ miles from the canal's entrance at Rotherhithe. The Act of Parliament required mile posts to be erected at $\frac{1}{2}$ mile intervals so that tolls could be correctly calculated.

← The site of Peckham Basin and Wharf in 1987. Comparison with the previous photograph shows that some of the buildings were still standing but were about to be demolished.

WANDSWORTH CANAL
(Alias MacMURRAY'S CANAL)

The Act of Parliament authorizing the Surrey Iron Railway (1801) provided for a 'navigable communication between the river Thames and the said railway at Wandsworth'. The canal basin built at Ram Field was some 400 yards long. It could hold over thirty barges and was connected to the river by a tide-lock. It was opened in 1802. After the railway (q.v. the Croydon Canal) was closed in 1846, the ten acre dock was sold to Watney & Wells, the brewers. In 1865 the basin was being used for unloading esparto grass for the Royal Paper Mills in Garratt Lane and was known as MacMurray's Canal. In later years the dock was used by the Wandsworth, Wimbledon & Epsom District Gas Company who closed the lock in 1923 and filled in part of the basin in the 1930's. The part of the basin owned by the brewery was also filled in by 1940.

66. The Surrey Iron Railway Wharf at Ram Field Basin, Wandsworth, c. 1820, looking north towards the Thames from a point above the head of the dock where, behind the swing bridge, a barge is moored. Note the different types of waggon in use. Next to the cranes there was a turntable on roller bearings used for turning the waggons on to a stage projecting over the wharf, from which their contents could be tipped directly into barges.

Map overleaf

The 25" survey of 1866 shows the basin and canal at its fullest extent. Later editions show six gasometers, three on each side of the northern swing bridge. The tide lock linking the canal to the River Thames is shown at the top of the map.

WEY NAVIGATION

The River Wey was made navigable from its junction with the Thames at Weybridge to Guildford under an Act of 1651. The initiative had been taken by Sir Richard Weston of Sutton Place in the 1630s when he had erected a pound lock at Stoke but further work had to be postponed until after the end of the Civil War. Although the navigation was completed in 1653 at a cost of £15,000, tiresome disputes over compensation and ownership nearly closed the waterway in the 1670s. After these had finally been settled, barge traffic rapidly increased and Guildford prospered as it supplied the London markets with agricultural produce and a host of manufactured items which included beer, flour, paper and wooden goods. Daniel Defoe remarked in 1724 that the navigation was a mighty support to the corn-market at Farnham and that timber came not only from the neighbourhood but from the woody parts of Sussex and Hampshire, thirty miles away. For that decade annual tolls averaged £2200 and the tonnage around 17,000. By 1800 this had increased to £5860 and 57,500 tons, a figure which was surpassed after the opening of the Wey & Arun Junction Canal (1816) by a peak of £7763 and 86003 tons in 1838. Thereafter improved road transport and the coming of the railway (it reached Guildford in 1845) saw traffic gradually decrease, eg:-

1860	£3001	60707 tons
1870	£2083	41585 tons
1880	£1549	29414 tons
1890	£1136	24581 tons
1900	£896	28297 tons

There was then a minor revival which saw tolls reaching £1981 in 1927 (55,622 tons) and £1398 in 1948 (25,334 tons). However the collapse of traffic on the Basingstoke Canal coupled with the decline of traffic to the London Docks and the flexibility and increased carrying power of road transport, finally removed the last commercial traffic in July 1969. In the meantime ownership of the navigation had been transferred to the National Trust who are encouraging pleasure boating and are able to maintain the waterway from revenue generated by land and mooring rents, visitors passes and annual licence fees which nowadays replace lock tolls.

67. Barges moored below Thames Lock waiting to enter the Wey Navigation in 1929.

68. Entrance to Thames Lock, Weybridge 1804 from a water-colour in Weybridge Museum.

69. The lock house at Thames Lock c. 1910. Edward Grove was lock-keeper from 1895 until 1939.

70. Thames Lock, Weybridge, 1950. Barge captain Stan Ellis stands on the barge as Len Turner, his mate, watches the horses from the bank. Pairs of horses towed the barges of William Stevens & Sons until 1960 when a tug was used to little advantage since tug and barge had to proceed singly through the locks.

71. The Oil Mills and Thames Lock c. 1920. In the 19th Century the mills were used to process rape seed for lighting and linseed for paint manufacture; the by-products were used for cattle cake.

BASINGSTOKE

72. The narrow boat **Basingstoke** loaded with coal and tied up above Thames Lock on the Wey. Weybridge Oil Mills can be seen in the background: Linseed was carried here by barge, until the mill was burnt down in 1963. **Basingstoke** was owned by the Woking, Aldershot & Basingstoke Canal Navigation Company in the 1880s and sold in 1893 to the Nately Brick & Tile Company for carrying their products to Ash Wharf, to Basingstoke and to other wharves along the canal. In 1907 they sold it to A.J. Harmsworth who used it as a lightening boat, to carry sand, round timber and coal, the last to Woking Gas Works. Between 1912 and 1914 Alec Harmsworth used **Basingstoke** in his historic attempt to delay abandonment of the western end of the Basingstoke Canal, by navigating its full length. In 1933 **Basingstoke** was taken to Ash Vale, and its iron frames were removed and used to build the barge **Brookwood**. Its remains can still be seen in Great Bottom Flash (see photograph no. 38).

74. In the nineteenth century the locks on the navigation had to be opened with a crowbar, three feet long. The hatches of many of them were placed in the centre of the gates so that it was necessary to sit astride, place the point of the crowbar in the niches of the hatch and by a series of violent jerks raise it – a far from easy task even when standing on terra firma. In 1867 J. B. Dashwood, the pleasure boat writer found the hatches very stiff and difficult and remarked that if the crowbar slipped out of its niche when the wrench was being made, away goes the unfortunate being into the water. One wonders if this might not have happened to John MacGregor of Rob Roy canoe fame. He wrote copiously about his voyages but when he passed through the Wey the year after Dashwood he only wrote three words in his diary – 'Adventures in locks', which suggests he might have suffered what Dashwood managed to avoid.

73. Barges lying at the oil mills above Thames Lock in 1959. Horse towage ceased in 1960.

75. The West County barge **Perseverance** at Coxes Mill in 1885. Regular barge traffic continued to the mill from London Docks until July 1969 when William Stevens & Sons were forced to cease trading with the removal of the grain terminals to Tilbury Docks.

76. Empty grain barges at Coxes Lock Mill, Weybridge, 1965. The last regular commercial traffic ceased on 4 July 1969 when *Perseverance* and *Speedwell* delivered the last cargoes of grain.

77. A Renault on the tow-path by Pyrford Lock in the 1920's. Note the turf sided lock. William Stevens & Sons barge in background.

78. Newark Mill in 1957. One of the finest water-mills in Southern England, it was burnt down in the 1960's. No other Surrey mill had three separate giant water wheels or eight pairs of stones. J. Hillier ominously wrote in 1951 "surveying the vast interior, every inch of timber, dusty and dry, it is not difficult to understand why so very few buildings of its period and its construction have been preserved – sooner or later they must inevitably be destroyed by fire."

79. Looking downstream from Newark Lock in 1936. Only a short section of the turf sided pound had a timber guard rail.

By the Commiſſioners for Executing the Office of Lord High Admiral of Great-Britain, *and* Ireland, *&c. And of all His Majeſty's Plantations*, &c.

YOU are hereby Required and Directed not to Impreſs into His Majeſty's Service George Wood employed in navigating a Barge on the River Wey & from Godalmin & Guilford and from the River Wey to London and back in the River Thames provided he is no Seaman and provided his Name, Age, and Deſcription, be inſerted in the Margin hereof, and that he does not belong to any of His Majeſty's Ships. And in Caſe this Protection ſhall be found about any other Perſon, producing the ſame upon his own Account, then the Officer who finds it, is hereby ſtrictly charged and required to Impreſs the ſaid Perſon, and immediately to ſend the Protection to Us. And we do hereby direct, That this Protection, for the Securing the forementioned Perſon, and him only, from the Preſs, ſhall continue in Force for Three Months. Given under our Hands, and the Seal of the Office of Admiralty, this Sixth Day of November One Thouſand Seven Hundred and SEVENTY- Six

George Wood, is about Five Feet Five Inches and a half High Aged Fifty years of a Fair Complexion and Wears his own Hair, has Lost the First Joynt of his Middle Finger on his Right hand

To all Commanders and Officers of His Majeſty's Ships, Preſs-Maſters, and all others whom it doth or may concern.

Sandwich

J Buller.

By Command of their Lordſhips,

Geo Jackson

[illegible]

Bargemen working on the Wey were liable to be victims of press gangs which operated until 1815. It was therefore necessary to obtain protection for individual bargemen from the Lords Commissioners of the Admiralty. Thirty five applications were made by the proprietors towards the end of the eighteenth century. Protections were only issued for three months and after they had expired, the petition pointed out 'the men have left their barges and secret themselves to avoid being pressed, whereby the trade is stopped to the very great detriment of the petitioners as well as the country in general.'

80. Turf-sided Newark Lock under repair in 1966.

81. Early form of lock construction: a turf-sided chamber at Paper Court Lock, near Old Woking, Surrey 1957. Similar turf-sided locks were to be found on the River Kennet in Berkshire.

82. Walter Grove, master carpenter from 1885 until 1930. He lived with his family at Worsfold Flood Gates between Send Bridge and Triggs Lock.

84. Triggs Lock c. 1920. John Wye was lock-keeper from 1915 until 1933. His predecessor, another of the Grove family, held the post for 59 years.

83. The Master Carpenter's workshop as it was in 1964.

85. A laden Thames barge approaching Guildford 1842. The Pewley Hill semaphore which formed part of the Admiralty's London to Portsmouth telegraph system can be seen at top left. It was in use from 1822 to 1847. The house remains occupied and is known today as Semaphore House. In favourable conditions a short message took about 15 minutes to pass the whole distance.

86. Dapdune Wharf in 1954. The boat building and repair shed can be seen at the end of the cut on the right. This was the navigation's main boatyard and had been in use since the 17th century.

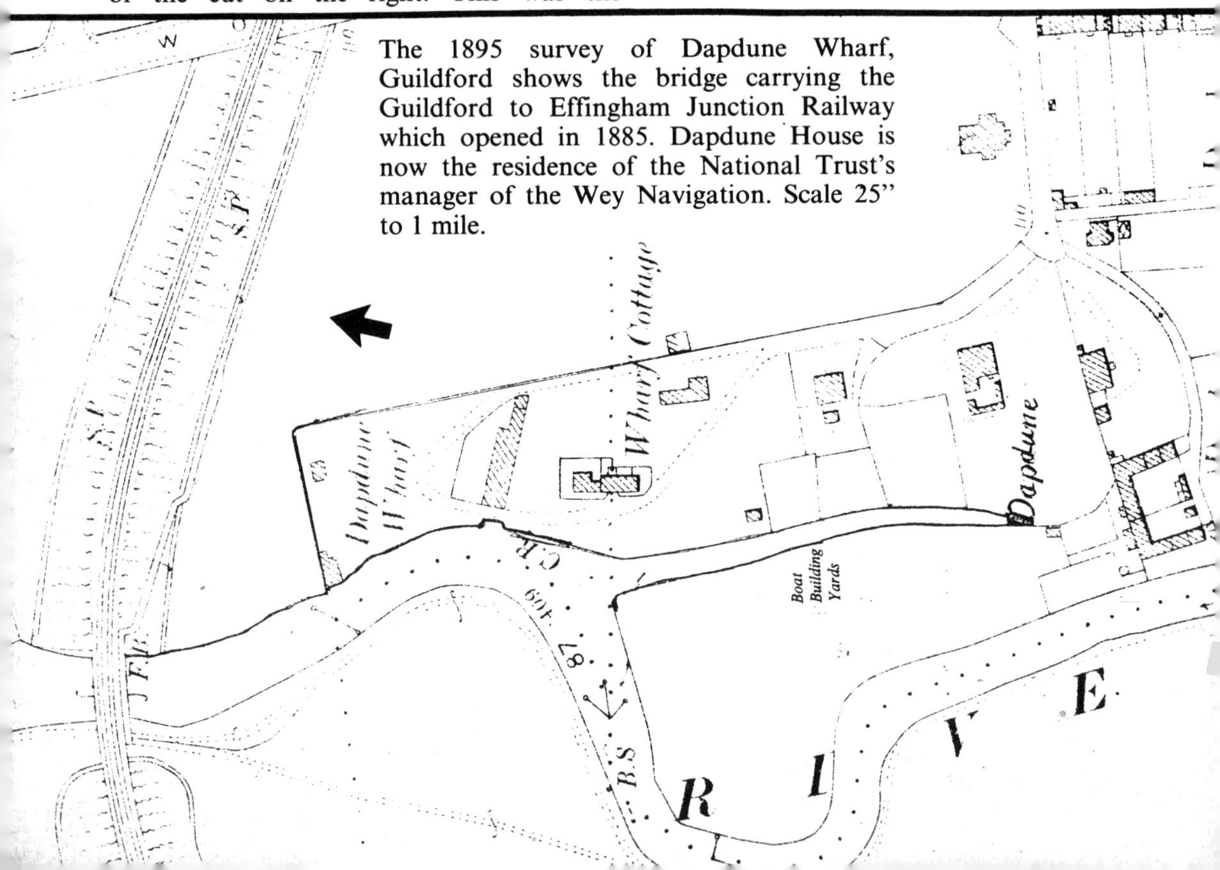

The 1895 survey of Dapdune Wharf, Guildford shows the bridge carrying the Guildford to Effingham Junction Railway which opened in 1885. Dapdune House is now the residence of the National Trust's manager of the Wey Navigation. Scale 25" to 1 mile.

87. **Reliance** being built at Dapdune Wharf Guildford in 1936 by Messrs. William Stevens & Sons. 72' 6" in length with a carrying capacity of 84 tons, she carried wheat and timber between Guildford and London until 1958.

88. Barges could be loaded and unloaded at Elkins coal wharf off Friary Street, Guildford by a crane which was operated by a tread-wheel 18 feet in diameter. The crane lay to the right of the moored barge in this 1860's view. Crooke's Brewery is on the left.

89. The crane was capable of lifting 3 tons at a time under the combined force of eight men. It was in use for more than a century and was last used in 1908 to unload concrete piles brought up the river for the foundation of the Technical Institute.

90. The wheel in detail. The crane and its wheel have been restored and re-erected between the two road bridges in Guildford town centre.

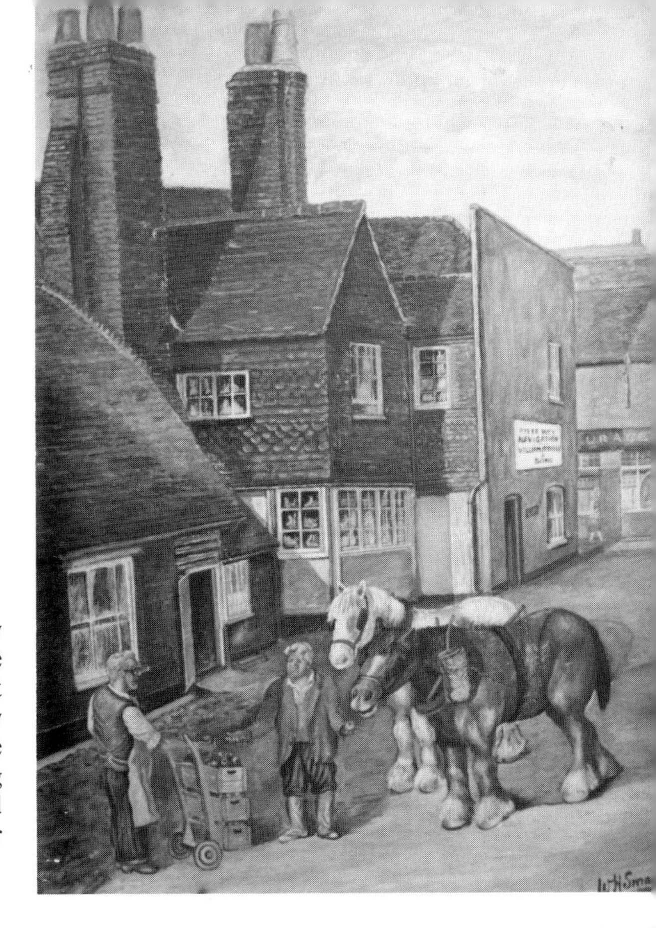

91. The Wey Navigation Offices off Friary Street Guildford in 1964. They were demolished to make way for a supermarket in 1970. The stables and store sheds lay between these and the river and these were demolished at the same time. The painting was by W. H. Smart and it was he who did much of the navigation's clerical work for many years.

92. Harry Stevens proprietor of the Navigation from 1930 until 1965. Before his death in 1970, he had ensured the future of the navigation by having its ownership transferred to the National Trust. The Stevens family had been connected with the navigation since Stevens great grandfather began work at Thames Lock in 1820.

WEY & ARUN JUNCTION CANAL

The Wey & Arun Junction Canal linked the Wey Navigation at Shalford with the Arun Canal at Newbridge near Wisborough Green thus providing an inland water route from the Thames at Weybridge to the English Channel at Littlehampton. Although an attempt to link the rivers Wey and Arun had been made in 1641 the Parliamentary bill failed to pass through the House of Lords (see London's Lost Route to the Sea chapter III) and it was not until 1813 that an Act of Parliament was obtained. The canal was surveyed by Josias Jessop, a son of William Jessop and constructed first by Zachariel Keppel, a local contractor of Alfold who went bankrupt and then completed by May Upton, the Petworth surveyor.

The canal was opened for traffic on 29 September 1816. Its total length was 18½ miles and the main engineering works consisted of 18 locks, over 30 bridges and two small aqueducts at Bramley and Drungewick. Besides serving the villages of Bramley, Wonersh, Cranleigh, Alfold, Dunsfold and Loxwood, it formed the only inland water link between the Thames and the English Channel.

The cost of building the canal was £107,000; £99,550 was raised by the issue of 905 shares of £100 at £110 each and the balance by mortgaging the tolls. The largest shareholder was George O'Brien Wyndham, the 3rd Earl of Egremont who held 250 shares or 28 per cent of the equity. The highest dividend paid on the £100 shares was 1%; the last of 6/- per cent was distributed in May 1866.

Barges from the coast brought seaweed for the farms, grain for the watermills, coal for the gasworks and a wide variety of groceries and merchandise for the village stores; they returned loaded with bark, farm produce, flour, forest timber and items like hoops and the other products of rural industry. Local traffic consisted mainly of chalk, clay, sand and gravel from the pits to the kilns and wharves at villages and farms. Exceptionally, the waterway from Portsmouth to London saw barges guarded by red coats carrying bullion to the Bank of England; more frequent were the cargoes of eggs, wine, old rope, rags and soldiers' baggage. Occasionally their manifest showed oddities like acorns, bullock horns, burr stones, carrots, cyder and fruit.

The tonnage carried was never substantial. It averaged only 9,000 tons until the opening of the Portsmouth & Arundel Canal in 1823 when it rose to an average of 16,000 tons during the next seven years.

In spite of the virtual demise of the London to Portsmouth trade the average exceeded 18,500 tons during the 1830's. Although the peak tonnage of 23,250 in 1839–40 was never surpassed, it did not drop below 10,000 tons until after the opening of the Guildford-Horsham Railway in 1865. An Act of Abandonment was obtained after much difficulty in 1868 which allowed the canal to be officially closed on 22 July 1871.

Barges however continued to trade to Bramley Wharf until 27 June 1872. The land and buildings belonging to the canal company were gradually sold back to the riparian owners.

Although many writers and countryside explorers have bewailed the loss of this waterway over the past eighty years, serious efforts to reopen the canal only began in 1970 with the formation of The Wey & Arun Canal Society, later to become the Wey & Arun Canal Trust. It now has 700 members and has successfully raised money through sponsored walks, jumble sales and from donations. The Trust has been responsible for clearing and dredging five miles of the canal bed, putting Rowner and Mallam locks back into working order and rebuilding numerous bridges and culverts. The Shalford Natural History Society cleared and repaired Tanyard Bridge at Gosden in 1977. Similarly the Pulborough Society was among those who contributed to the cost of rebuilding Pallingham Quay Bridge which was reopened in 1976. Before the line of the former waterway can be restored however, formidable difficulties remain to be overcome since some landowners who now own some 13 miles of the canal bed do not wish a public right of way to divide their land. The fact that a large housing estate has been built upon the canal bed at Bramley will also necessitate a new line of waterway being cut. The prospects for the navigation being fully restored are therefore uncertain. Much will depend on the results of a cost feasibility study currently being undertaken, the attitude of the Surrey and West Sussex County Councils, the Southern Water Authority, the forty or so riparian landowners and the continued enthusiasm of the many voluntary workers who have already been toiling amidst the undergrowth and mire for more than a decade.

Illustrations of the Southern part of the Wey & Arun Junction Canal appear in *West Sussex Waterways* (Middleton Press 1985)

93. The approach to the first bridge over the waterway at Shalford in 1952. The stream here was widened and dredged in 1815 and the canal itself was dug from stonebridge.

94. The approach to the site of Stonebridge Lock in 1952. The foot bridges link the gardens of the private residences which are divided by the old canal.

95. The bridge over the canal at Gosden Common, Bramley in 1964. When the Guildford to Horsham railway was opened in 1865 the road bridge over the railway was extended over the canal (far parapet) and incorporated the canal bridge, built in 1815, which enabled horses to cross from one side of the tow-path to the other.

96. The Shalford Conservation Society restored the brickwork and cleared the heavily overgrown site. Here the author is seen taking part in the reopening ceremony held in October 1977.

97. The Guildford–Horsham railway at Gosden running parallel to the former channel of the canal, 1964. The canal bridge is centre right with the tanyard behind. The railway was closed in 1965.

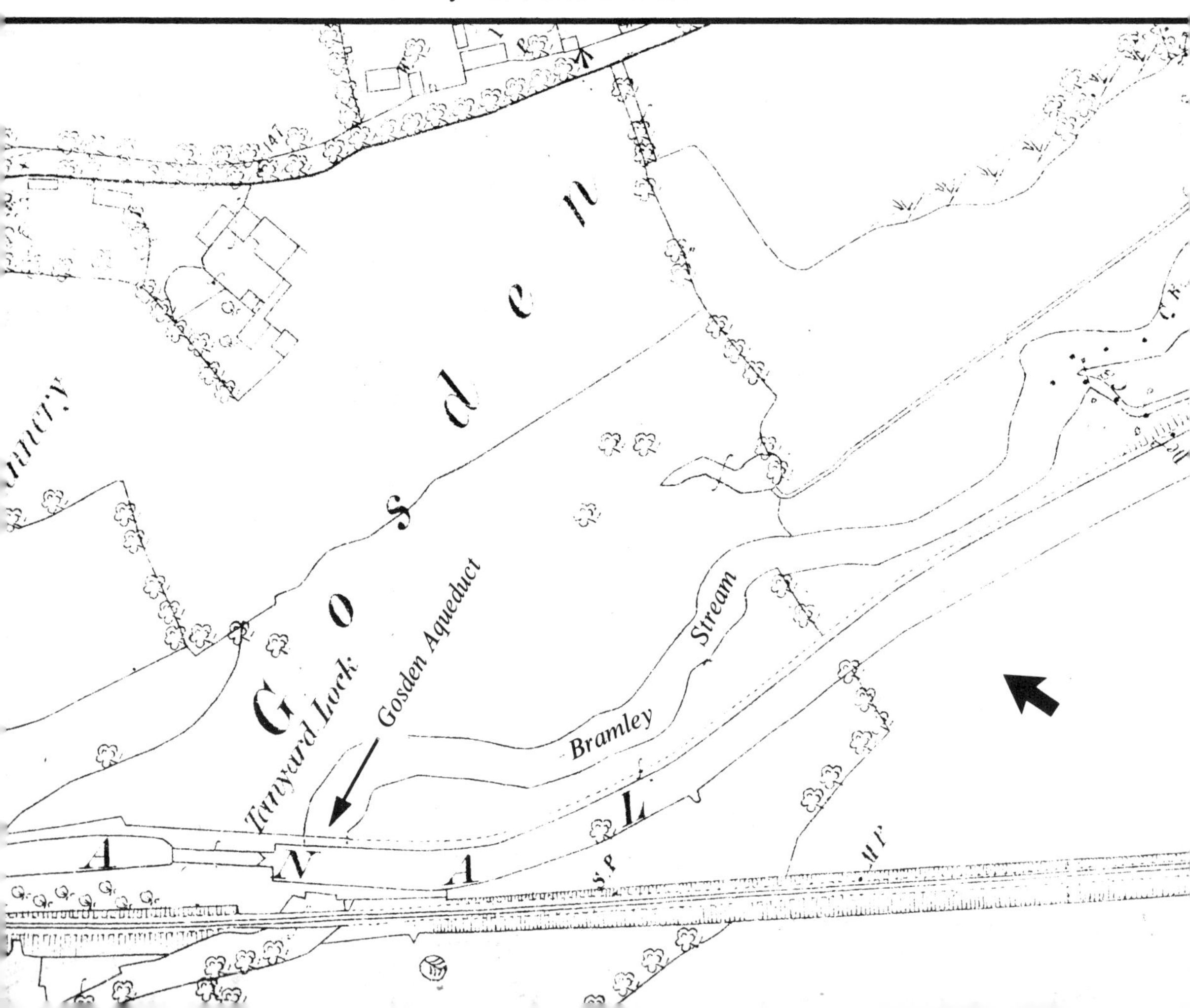

98. Gosden Aqueduct, which carried the canal over the Bramley Stream, was immediately to the south of Tanyard Lock. The brick aqueduct was the first to be built in Surrey. Its bed and the channel between Summersbury Tannery and the lock were filled in before 1895. This view was taken in 1964.

1870 map at 25" to 1 mile. (The publishers apologise for unavoidably abbreviating the word CANAL)

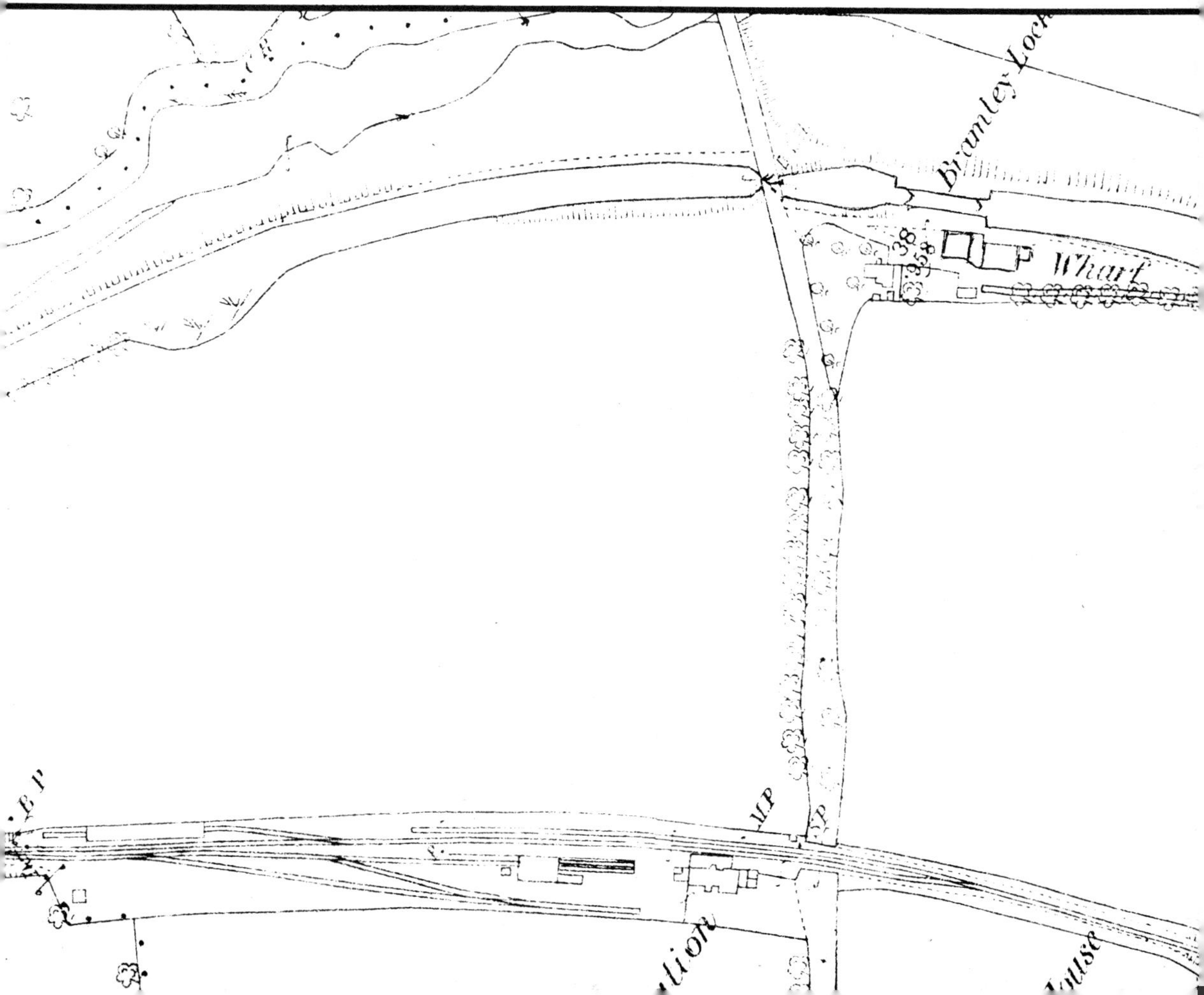

99. Coal merchant William Stanton who was lock-keeper at Bramley (1849–1871) and superintendant of the northern end of the canal (1867–1871). When he died aged 61 his obituary referred to his many admirable traits of character and acts of benevolence, one of which was to allow author and pleasure boater, J. B. Dashwood 'the run of his kitchen garden, rich in gooseberries and currants'. The edge of Bramley lock is visible in the foreground with the wharf cottage behind, c. 1870.

Lord & Lady Grantley ***with*** **Mr. C. F. Norton** ***request the Pleasure of*** *the two Miss Talbots'* ***Company to a Fête Champêtre, at Wonersh, on Thursday, the 26th Instant, at Two o'Clock.***

Wonersh, 18th May, 1831.

**** It is requested that this Card may be delivered at the Porter's Lodge.*

☞ Boats will be provided to convey the Company to Wonersh, and will start from Guildford Bridge at One o'Clock precisely.

N. B.---In the event of the Day fixed for the Fête proving unfavorable, it will be postponed to the following Day.

Skinner, Columbian Press, Guildford.

The invitation to the two Miss Talbots' stated that boats would be provided to convey the party to Wonersh and would start from Guildford Bridge at one o'clock precisely. Whether the canal was used on more than one occasion by Lord and Lady Grantley is not known nor what type of boat was used for such an event.

100. The 1952 view shows some changes to the house.

101. The canal bed in 1952 where it formerly passed through Lord Grantley's Park in Wonersh and now forms part of the gardens of houses on the Linersh Wood Estate.

WEY and ARUN JUNCTION CANAL.

WITH ADVANTAGE OF WATER CARRIAGE.

THE USEFUL

MATERIALS

OF TWO

WINDMILL PUMPS,

Situate on the Banks of the Wey and Arun Junction Canal, in the respective Parishes of Bramley and Cranley, near Guildford, Surrey.

To be sold by Auction (by order of the Committee of Management of the Wey and Arun Junction Canal Company) by Mr.

FREDK KEENE

SUCCESSOR TO THE LATE MR. LOMAS,

AT THE JOLLY FARMER INN, BRAMLEY, SURREY,

ON TUESDAY, DECEMBER 6, 1853,

AT TWO O'CLOCK.

BIRTLEY MILL.

LOT 1.
All the useful Machinery, Sails, Fans, and Gear of Windmill (as marked) with the stout oak frame work, Cowl, &c.

LOT 2.
Two 12-inch double Cylinder Pumps, with iron Beam, Bearer, &c.

LOT 3.
All the Brickwork Erection of Mill and Shaft (as marked) with Door and Frame.

CRANLEY MILL.

LOT 4.
All the useful Machinery, Sails, Fans, and Gear of Windmill (as marked) with the stout oak Frame-work, Cowl, &c., &c.

LOT 5.
Two 12-inch double Cylinder Pumps with iron Beam, Bearer, &c.

LOT 6.
All the Brickwork Erection of Mill and Shaft as marked.

The Properties may be viewed Two Days prior to the Sale, and Catalogues had at the Jolly Farmer, Bramley; Onslow Arms, Cranley, and of Mr. FREDERICK KEENE, Auctioneer, Estate Agent, and Valuer, 19, North Street, Guildford, Surrey.

(RUSSELLS, PRINTERS, &c., GUILDFORD.)

102. Primitive foot-bridge across the Birtley channel in 1946.

103. The grass grown dried-up channel at Rushett Common in 1952 where the canal ran parallel to the Guildford–Horsham railway. The two carriage train is drawn by a former L.B. & S.C.R. tank engine built in the 1880s. On the site of the parish boundary, i.e. where some buildings stand above the engine's chimney, stood James Tickner's vinegar works in the mid-19th century. This was one of the few local industries to be attracted to the canal's banks.

104. In spite of the efforts made by the Wey & Arun Canal Trust to dredge the canal, until the channel can be refilled with water, weeds soon choke the bed as this 1987 scene of the waterway north of the main road at Run Common shows.

105. Run Common Wharf 1952. Close at hand on Run Common was the charcoal furnace belonging to Richard Medland which burnt some 2,000 tons of cordwood annually to manufacture naphtha, acetic acid, and some 500 tons of charcoal. These products were rarely sold locally and had to be taken by water to Littehampton from where they were shipped to London. As local timber became scarce difficulty was experienced in obtaining wood from further afield. Timber bought at Slinfold had, for instance, to be either carted to Newbridge or to Loxwood and loaded into barges bound for Run Common.

106. Iron swing bridge at Whipley Manor, 1952.

107. Lock XVII as abandoned to nature in 1963.

108. Restoration of Lock XVII was well advanced when photographed in 1982. The Wey & Arun Trust's voluntary working parties laboured hard and by 1986 the lock had been rebuilt.

WEY & ARUN NAVIGATION.

£5 REWARD

WHEREAS, on Sunday the 13th day of August instant, a quantity of the COPING on ELM BRIDGE was maliciously removed and injured;

NOTICE IS HEREBY GIVEN, that any Person who will give Information to Mr. STANTON, the Superintendent of the Navigation, so as to lead to the Conviction of the Offender or Offenders, shall receive a Reward of £5.

W. HAYDON SMALLPEICE,
CLERK.

Guildford,
15th August, 1848.

(Russells, Printers and Stationers.)

109. The superintendant's cottage at Elmbridge Wharf, Cranleigh. Thomas Pullen lived here in the 1860s and was alleged, in the course of evidence heard by the House of Lords Committee considering the bill for the canal's abandonment in 1868, to have "kept a shop or something of that kind" and whose services were "entirely useless".

112. Mill Farm, Hascombe (1952 view) stands on the banks of the canal and on the other side to the former mill stream emanating from Vachery Pond. There is no evidence of when the mill ceased to function but it seems possible that it was before the canal was opened in 1816 since it does not appear in the schedule of buildings effected by the line of the proposed canal nor has any reference been found of the canal company paying compensation. Certainly there is no trace of the mill race and sluices which suggests the mill may have ceased to operate before the canal was built.

←

110 and 111. Changing views of the Summit Level near Cranleigh during the summer and winter of 1952.

113. The brick work visible in this 1964 view indicates the remains of a wharf.

114. Overspill weir from the canal's summit level south of Mill Farm passing beneath the tow-path in 1964 and flowing into the Bramley Stream. In times of abnormally heavy rainfall a constant watch would be maintained to ensure that the paddles were sufficiently raised to prevent the canal banks bursting or overflowing.

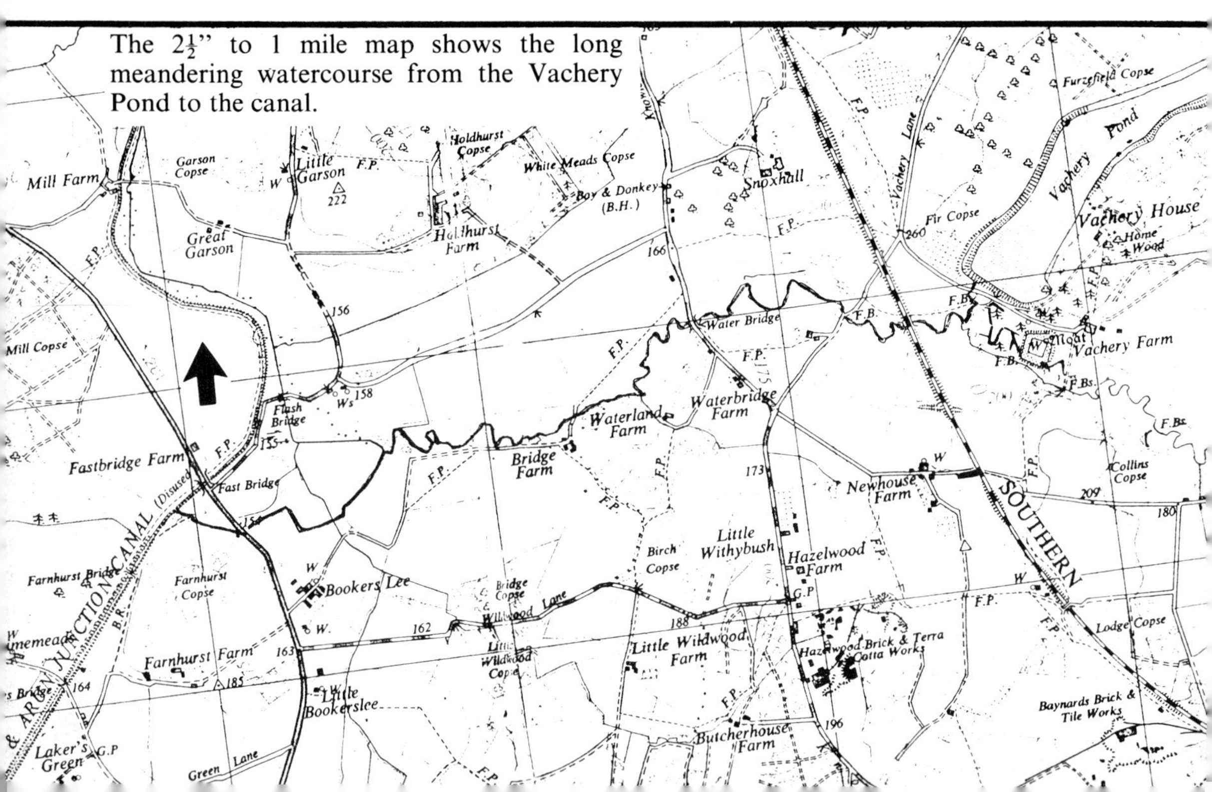

The $2\frac{1}{2}$" to 1 mile map shows the long meandering watercourse from the Vachery Pond to the canal.

115. The point south of Fastbridge where the $2\frac{1}{2}$ mile feeder conduit from the 40 acre Vachery Pond Reservoir flowed into the canal (1964). It is still functional but was inadequate to maintain the five mile summit level in dry spells; even when the reservoir was full the difference in water levels was little more than 20 feet. As it was the only regular source of supply (the remainder coming from springs and field drains) when the reservoir level fell, barges had to be lightened by transfering goods to lighters or to land carriage between Cranleigh and Alfold. The erection of two pump windmills by locks XVII and XVIII in the 1830's only partially alleviated the problem.

116. It was at the Compasses Inn Alfold on 29th September 1816 that the Earl· of Egremont accompanied by numeous friends and shareholders, attended by the mayor and aldermen of Guildford, assembled to celebrate the official opening of the waterway. A processing of barges left Compasses Bridge for Guildford while outside the inn the navigators devoured a roasted ox and drank two hundred gallons of ale. (1964 photo).

117. The summit pound from Compasses Bridge, Alfold 1934. After over sixty years disuse, exploring the old canal had became a pastime for nature lovers. On 4 September 1936 **The Times** published a nostalgic article on the canal and included on the back page a half page photograph showing the lily covered channel as viewed here.

The 1895 revision of the 25 inch survey shows the weeds beginning to encroach upon the west side of Ticknersheath Bridge. Cobden's Farm had its own private wharf at which timber and agricultural produce were regularly loaded. Opposite were the brickworks established when the canal was being built in 1814.

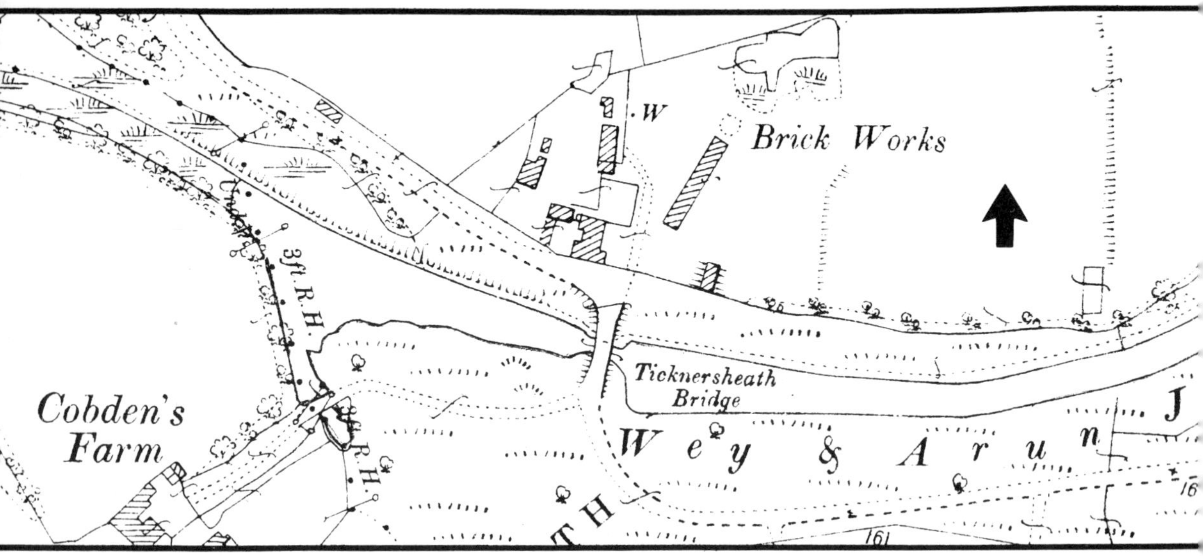

118. Alfold Mill c. 1905. The smock mill stood above the cutting on the east bank of the canal between Compasses and Simmond's bridges. It operated between 1820 and 1870 and was demolished in 1913. It has yet to be established whether there was a tunnel leading from the canal into the base of the mill or whether barges were loaded by crane or chute since the water level was some distance below the ground level of the mill.

119. After the canal was closed in 1871, the official liquidator attempted to sell back the land to the riparian owners. By 1901 he had succeeded in getting rid of all but 8 of the 200 acres but when the company was finally dissolved in 1910, there was still no indication of whether seven remaining parcels of land had found purchasers. The above stretch near Ticknersheath appeared to have no owner in 1952 although occupied by frogs, water lilies and all manner of water fowl.

120. The lock-house in Sydney Wood was adjacent to Lock XV and was also the Canal Company's main workshop. John Cole and his family lived there for over thirty years in the mid-nineteenth century carrying out all manner of repairs, constructing lock-gates and building boats.

The canal left Surrey between locks IX and VIII in Gennets Wood, a rural location about one mile from Alfold village. At this point it was 58¾ miles from London Bridge. 14 more locks had to be passed and 34 miles travelled before Littlehampton and the English Channel were reached. Mileposts had to erected every half mile along the canal banks to ensure correct calculation of the tolls. The post erected close to the county boundary showed that it was 11½ miles from the Wey at Shalford and 7 miles from the Arun Canal at Newbridge. It is thought that the actual posts were made of iron and inscribed as on the map. 25" scale 1870 survey.

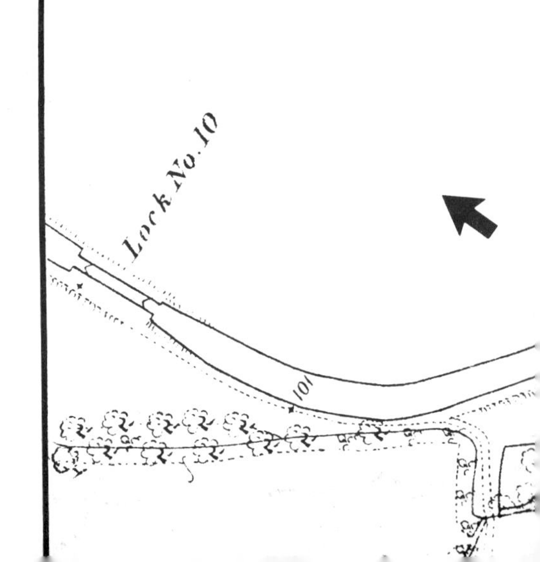

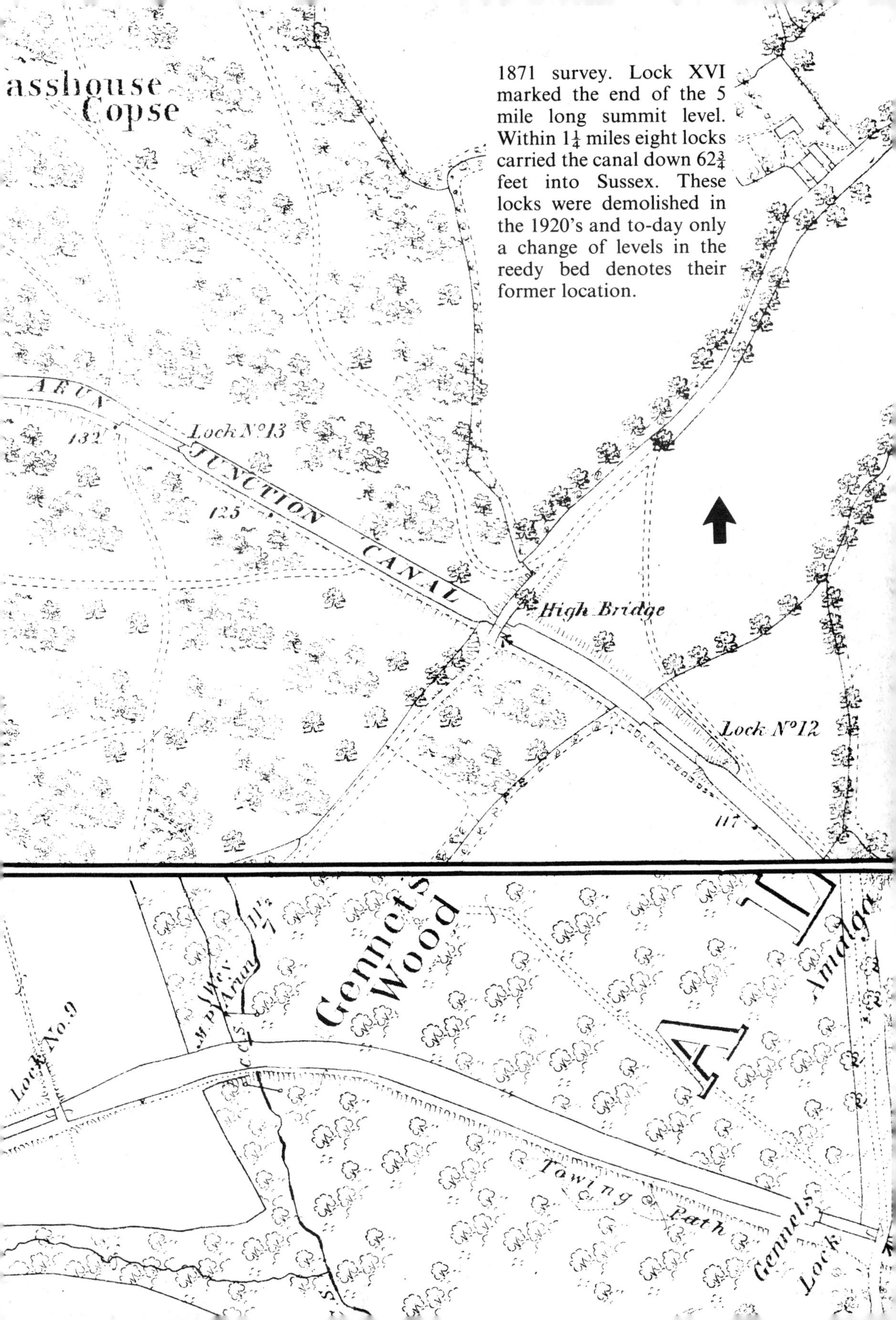

1871 survey. Lock XVI marked the end of the 5 mile long summit level. Within $1\frac{1}{4}$ miles eight locks carried the canal down $62\frac{3}{4}$ feet into Sussex. These locks were demolished in the 1920's and to-day only a change of levels in the reedy bed denotes their former location.

FURTHER READING

Basingstoke Canal Restoration 1985 D. Jebens and D. Robinson
Boats from the Basingstoke's Past 1969 A. Harmsworth
Canals to Croydon and Camberwell 1986 (Living History Publications and Environment Bromley)
Guide to the Basingstoke Canal 1984 R Cansdale and D. Jebens
London's Lost Route to Basingstoke 196 P.A.L. Vine
London's Lost Route to the Sea 1986 (4t edition) P.A.L. Vine
West Sussex Waterways 1985 P.A.L. Vine